CGP

11+ Verbal Reasoning

For the CEM test – ages 10-11

Preparing for CEM 11+ Verbal Reasoning can feel like a real challenge... but fear not! This CGP book is stuffed to bursting with the best revision and practice around!

It's got plenty of revision notes, top tips and excellent examples, as well as questions that are sure to test your knowledge and polish your skills.

Just when you thought that was it, there are also mixed practice tests, two test-style papers, and answers for every question. You'll certainly be raring to go on the big day.

How to access your free Online Edition

This book includes a free Online Edition to read on your PC, Mac or tablet. You'll just need to go to **cgpbooks.co.uk/extras** and enter this code:

1378 3495 5617 4278

By the way, this code only works for one person. If somebody else has used this book before you, they might have already claimed the Online Edition.

Complete
Revision & Practice

Everything you need to pass the test!

Contents

About the 11+

What's in the 11+ 1

What's in the 11+ Verbal Reasoning Test 2

How to Prepare for the 11+ 3

Section One — Spelling

Preparing for the Test 4

Plurals 6

Homophones and Homographs 8

Prefixes and Suffixes 10

Silent Letters and Double Letters 12

Other Awkward Spellings.. 14

Practice Questions.. 16

Section Two — Word Meanings

Preparing for Word Meaning Questions 22

Multiple Meanings 24

Closest Meaning 26

Opposite Meaning 30

Odd One Out 34

Reorder Words to Make a Sentence 36

Practice Questions.. 38

Section Three — Completing Passages

Preparing for Cloze Questions 44

Using Rules of English — Verbs.. 46

Using Rules of English — Conjunctions 48

Answering Cloze Questions.. 50

Practice Questions.. 54

Section Four — Comprehension

Reading the Text 62

Understanding the Questions.. 64

Finding Hidden Facts 66

Understanding the Language in the Text.. 68

Multiple Statement Questions — Logic 71

Word Meanings 74

Reasoning Questions 76

Answering Comprehension Questions 78

Practice Questions 80

Mixed Practice Tests.. 88

Test-Style Paper 1 100

Test-Style Paper 2 112

Glossary 124

Answers... 125

Index 140

Published by CGP

Editors:
Keith Blackhall, Claire Boulter, Emma Cleasby, Rebecca Greaves,
Holly Robinson, Rebecca Russell and Matt Topping.

With thanks to Tom Carney for the proofreading.
With thanks to Lottie Edwards for the copyright research.

Every effort has been made to locate copyright holders and obtain permission to reproduce sources. For those sources
where it has been difficult to trace the originator of the work, we would be grateful for information. If any copyright
holder would like us to make an amendment to the acknowledgements, please notify us and we will gladly update the
book at the next reprint. Thank you.

ISBN: 978 1 78908 597 6

Printed by Elanders Ltd, Newcastle upon Tyne.
Clipart from Corel®

What's in the 11+

Here's a quick overview of what's in the 11+ to help you get your head round the basics.

The 11+ is an Admissions Test

1) The 11+ is a test used by some schools to help with their selection process.
2) You'll usually take it when you're in Year 6, at some point during the autumn term.
3) Schools use the results to decide who to accept. They might also use other things to help make up their mind, like information about where you live.

> If you're unsure, ask your parents to check when you'll be taking your 11+ tests.

You'll be tested on a Mixture of Subjects

1) In your 11+, you'll be tested on these subjects:

| Maths | Verbal Reasoning | This tests reading comprehension, vocabulary and spelling. |

Non-Verbal Reasoning — This tests your ability to solve problems involving pictures and diagrams.

> If you're not sitting the CEM test, you might get a different mixture of subjects. Make sure you know which test is used by the school you're applying for.

2) You'll probably sit two 45 minute tests, each made up of a mixture of subjects.
3) This book will help you with the Verbal Reasoning part of the test.

Get to Know what Kinds of Questions you might get

Most of the questions in your test will be multiple choice but for some you might have to write your answer yourself.

> Look out for the tips in each section — they'll give you practical advice about the test, plus revision tips and extra hints to help you crack 11+ Verbal Reasoning.

Multiple Choice

1) For each question you'll be given some options on the question paper.
2) You should draw a clear pencil line in the box next to the option that you think is correct.
3) You might have to mark your answers on a separate answer sheet.

Fill in the Blanks

You'll have to fill in some boxes to answer these questions. Here's an example:

> Complete the word on the right so that it means the opposite of the word on the left.
>
> smooth   r [ ] [ ] g [ ]

Just write the letters neatly inside the boxes.

What's in the 11+ Verbal Reasoning Test

Get your brain ready for Verbal Reasoning by reading about the different question types.

Verbal Reasoning tests your Reading and Word Knowledge

1) You'll already have picked up loads of the skills you need at school.
2) There are four main types of questions that can crop up:

Spelling and Grammar

You might be asked to proofread a passage — you'll have to spot and correct spelling and grammar mistakes.

Word Meanings

These questions test your vocabulary and word knowledge. Questions of this type will ask you to think about the meanings of words or find connections between them.

Cloze Passages

It's likely that you'll be given one long or several short cloze passages in your test. Each cloze passage is a text with some bits missing. You'll either have to choose some words to fill the gaps, or fill in the missing letters in some of the words. To do this you'll need to be able to spell words correctly, and have a good grasp of grammar.

Comprehension

You'll probably be given one long text or several short texts to read. You'll have to answer questions which test how well you understand the text. The questions might ask you about:
- what the text means — what happens in the text, what a character is like or how they feel, or what the writer's purpose is.
- word meanings — what some of the trickier words in the text mean.

3) You might also get other types of question to test your word knowledge. For example, you could be asked to reorder words to make a sentence.
4) For all these types of question, it's important for you to have a good vocabulary and to understand how words and sentences are made.

How to Prepare for the 11+

Give yourself a head start with your Verbal Reasoning preparation — be organised and plan ahead.

Divide your Preparation into Stages

1) You should find a way to prepare for the 11+ that suits you. This may depend on how much time you have before the test. Here's a good way to plan your Verbal Reasoning revision:

> Use this book to revise strategies for answering different question types. Read through the study notes and follow the worked examples carefully — make sure you understand the method used at each step.

> Do plenty of practice questions, concentrating on the question types you find tricky.

> Sit some practice papers to prepare yourself for the real test.

2) When you first start answering Verbal Reasoning questions, try to solve the questions without making any mistakes, rather than working quickly.

3) Once you feel confident about the questions, then you can build up your speed.

4) You can do this by asking an adult to time you as you answer a set of questions, or by seeing how many questions you can answer in a certain amount of time, e.g. 5 minutes. You can then try to beat your time or score.

5) As you get closer to the test day, work on getting a balance between speed and accuracy — that's what you're aiming for when you sit the real test.

There are Many Ways to Practise the Skills you Need

The best way to tackle Verbal Reasoning is to do lots of revision and practice. This isn't the only thing that will help though — there are other ways you can hone the skills you need for the test:

1) Read a mix of fiction and non-fiction — poetry, newspapers, novels etc.
2) If you come across any unfamiliar words, look them up in a dictionary. Keeping a vocabulary list is a great way to remember new words.
3) If you're reading an article in a newspaper or magazine, underline the key facts as you read — picking out the most important information from a text is a really useful skill.
4) Play word games or do crosswords to build up your vocabulary.
5) Play games like 'Twenty Questions' or 'Cluedo' to help you think logically and draw conclusions based on information that you're given.

Preparing for the Test

Make sure you know how words are made — it'll help you in your test.

Lots of words follow **Spelling Rules**

Whether you're looking for spelling errors or completing words in a cloze question
(see Section Three), it'll help if you can recognise common spelling patterns.

Patterns at the **Start** of words

1) Words can start with any letter of the alphabet, but not any combination of letters.

2) You'll see 'b', 'c', 'f', 'g', 'p' or 't' before 'l' or 'r', but never after 'l' or 'r' at the start of a word.

blow, crown, flip, grab, plot, trip   lb✗ rb✗ lc✗ rc✗ lf✗ rf✗ lg✗ rg✗ lp✗ rp✗ rt✗

3) 'h' is common after 'c', 's', 't' and 'w'. ⟶ chip, shop, this, when

4) A prefix (see p.10) can be added to the start of a word to change its meaning, for example:

in- (inedible, indescribable)   dis- (disappear, dislike)

un- (unlock, untidy)

Patterns in the **Middle** of words

1) Almost all words contain vowels. Some patterns of vowels appear frequently, for example:

ee oo ou ie ea   seen look pout diet tear

2) Some vowels rarely appear together, for example, 'uo', 'iu', 'ae'.

3) Double consonants (see p.12) in the middle of words are common — you'll often come across 'tt', 'ss' or 'pp', but it's less likely you'll see a word with 'hh', 'vv', 'jj', 'ww' or 'xx'.

butter	cutting	letter
assume	vessel	issue
stopping	rapped	appear

4) If you can recognise common vowel and consonant patterns that appear in the middle of words, such as 'per', 'our', 'are' and 'ate', it'll help to improve your spelling.

Preparing for the Test

Patterns at the End of words

1) Some combinations of consonants are often found at the end of words. For example:

> church   clock   fifth   cash   harm   high   string

2) Suffixes (see p.10) come at the end of words — they can be verb endings like '-ed', plurals such as '-s' or adverb endings like '-ly'. Here are some common suffixes:

> -ition (addition)   -ity (humidity)   -ful (careful)   -ing (playing)   -y (sandy)

3) Remember, when you add a suffix the spelling of the root word can change:

> take ➡ takeing ✗ taking ✓   prepare ➡ prepareation ✗ preparation ✓

Use Spelling Patterns to help you answer questions

1) If you know a bit about prefixes it can help you work out the meaning of words, for example:

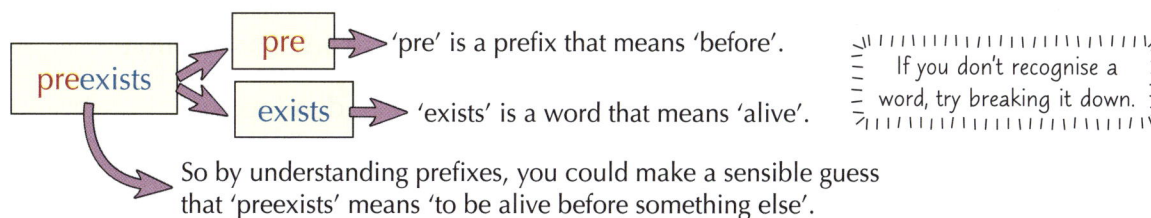

> preexists ➡ pre ➡ 'pre' is a prefix that means 'before'.
> exists ➡ 'exists' is a word that means 'alive'.
>
> *If you don't recognise a word, try breaking it down.*
>
> So by understanding prefixes, you could make a sensible guess that 'preexists' means 'to be alive before something else'.

2) Revise some common patterns in the middle of words — it'll help with your spelling.

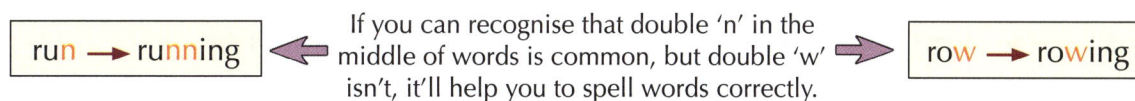

> run ➡ running   If you can recognise that double 'n' in the middle of words is common, but double 'w' isn't, it'll help you to spell words correctly.   row ➡ rowing

Practice Questions

1) Find three prefixes other than un-, dis- and in-.

2) Can you think of any words that start with the following letters?
   a) str   b) blr   c) shr   d) ds

3) Write the correct spelling of each of these words.
   a) anywere   b) stuborn   c) hovvercraft   d) shipwrec

4) Write out each of these root words with the prefix or suffix added.
   a) un + natural   b) angry + ly   c) mis + spell   d) vaccine + ate

A big vocabulary is a big help...

The more words you know, then the more familiar certain spelling patterns will become. Making sure you have a wide vocabulary will help you to identify correct spellings much more easily.

6

Plurals

Plural means 'more than one'. So here's a plural number of pages about plurals. Enjoy...

Add 's' to make Most Words plural

Most plurals are formed by adding an 's':

mask ⟶ masks   Monday ⟶ Mondays

Other words have Different Rules

Words that End in 'ch', 'sh', 's', 'x' and 'z'

1) Put 'es' at the end of words ending in these letters.
2) You need to add the 'es' to make sure that you keep the soft sound in the original word.

kiss ⟶ kisses

watch ⟶ watches

Words that End in 'o'

1) Words that end in 'o' usually need 's' to make their plural, e.g. pianos, discos.
2) Some of these words are different though — they take 'es' instead. For example:

potatoes   tomatoes   heroes   echoes   dominoes

Words that End in 'f' and 'fe'

1) You need to add 'ves' to many words that end in 'f' and 'fe' to make them plural.

loaf ⟶ loaves   shelf ⟶ shelves   wife ⟶ wives

2) But again, some are different. These words just need an 's':

chiefs   chefs   beliefs   reefs   giraffes   riffs

Words that End in 'y'

1) If the letter before the 'y' is a vowel, just add 's' to make the plural:

toy ⟶ toys

2) If the letter before the 'y' is a consonant, the 'y' becomes 'ies' for the plural:

daisy ⟶ daisies

> Vowels are the letters 'a', 'e', 'i', 'o' and 'u'. All the other letters of the alphabet are consonants.

Irregular Plurals

These words all change their vowel sound when they become plural:

tooth ⟶ teeth   woman ⟶ women   mouse ⟶ mice

man ⟶ men   goose ⟶ geese   oasis ⟶ oases

Section One — Spelling

Plurals

You may be asked to **Choose** the **Correct Plural**

EXAMPLE: **Circle the correct plural to complete each sentence below.**

a) My family owns three *stereoes / stereoss / stereos / steroes*.
b) The clown at the circus was juggling with *knifes / kniffs / knifies / knives*.
c) My sister still believes in *faires / fairies / fairys / faireys*.
d) We have *mouses / mice / mise / mousies* living under the floorboards.

Method — Follow the rules for making plurals

1) Follow the rules to work out the plurals.
2) Remember to look out for any exceptions to the rules (see the previous page).

a) My family owns three *stereoes / stereoss /*(*stereos*)*/ steroes*.

The word 'stereo' ends in 'o', so the plural ending has to be 's' or 'es'. → 'Stereo' takes the 's' ending — so the correct plural is 'stereos'.

b) The clown at the circus was juggling with *knifes / kniffs / knifies /*(*knives*).

'Knife' has an 'fe' ending. Many words ending in 'fe' take the plural 'ves', but some end in 's'. → The plural of 'knife' takes the more common 'ves' ending, so the answer is 'knives'.

c) My sister still believes in *faires /*(*fairies*)*/ fairys / faireys*.

'Fairy' ends with a 'y', so you need to look at the letter before the 'y' to work out the correct plural ending. → The letter before the 'y' is a consonant — 'r'. So the plural of 'fairy' is 'fairies'.

d) We have *mouses /*(*mice*)*/ mise / mousies* living under the floorboards.

The vowel sound of 'mouse' changes when it becomes plural. → The correct plural form of 'mouse' is 'mice'.

Practice Questions

1) Fill in the gap in each sentence, using the correct plural form of the word in brackets.

a) We watched the monkey swing from the _____ (branch) of the tree.

b) I always brush my _____ (tooth) twice a day.

c) We're spending Christmas with the _____ (Grady). ← *This one is asking for the plural of a name.*

d) I heard two _____ (wolf) howling in the forest.

e) Would you like to try on any of those _____ (dress)?

Revise the rules for forming plurals...

You might have to complete plurals in the test. You'll often be able to answer these questions by following the rules for forming plurals, but make sure you know the exceptions to the rules too.

Homophones and Homographs

Don't be put off by these complicated words — you probably know loads of homophones already.

Homophones sound the Same

1) Homophones are words that sound the same, but mean different things.
2) Here are lots of examples:

bean and been	root and route	weather and whether
pair and pear	rap and wrap	there, their and they're
wait and weight	blue and blew	by, buy and bye
maid and made	hire and higher	allowed and aloud
peer and pier	boy and buoy	principle and principal

Homographs have the Same Spelling

Homographs don't always sound the same.

1) Homographs are words that have the same spelling but a different meaning.
2) Here are some examples:

You need a bow and arrow to be an archer.

Remember that you must bow to the queen.

The word 'bow' has two different meanings in these sentences. You only know which meaning it is by reading the rest of the sentence.

The word 'wind' has different meanings, and it's pronounced differently in these two sentences.

The wind was howling round the house.

If you wind the handle it will play a tune.

A Pun is a Play on Words

Jokes that use homophones are called puns.

What do rabbits use to comb their fur? A hare brush.

Here 'hare' (an animal like a rabbit) is used instead of 'hair'. The two words are homophones.

I'm on a seafood diet — I see food and I eat it.

Seafood includes things like fish and prawns.

'See food' and 'seafood' are homophones.

Homophones and Homographs

Make sure you know the **Meanings** of common **Homophones**

EXAMPLE: **Circle the correct homophone to complete each sentence below.**

a) The supermarket is down by the *quay / key*.
b) My arm was feeling very *saw / sore* when I woke up this morning.
c) I can't *bear / bare* another day at school today.

Method — Look closely at the spelling of the homophones

1) Work out the <u>meaning</u> of the homophones in each sentence.
2) Then choose the <u>correct</u> homophone to <u>fit</u> the meaning of the sentence.

a) The supermarket is down by the (quay) / *key*.

A 'quay' is an area along a waterfront. It's somewhere that you may find a supermarket.

You open a lock using a 'key'. This meaning doesn't fit the sentence.

b) My arm was feeling very *saw* /(sore) when I woke up this morning.

'saw' could be the past tense of 'see' or a tool used for cutting wood.

'sore' means 'sensitive' and 'painful'. This is the correct answer — it fits in the sentence.

c) I can't (bear) / *bare* another day at school today.

'bear' is an animal, but it also means 'to endure' — this meaning fits the sentence.

'bare' means 'naked' or 'sparse'.

Be careful here — both 'bear' and 'saw' have several meanings. Don't let this confuse you.

Practice Questions

1) Circle the homophones that have been used incorrectly in the passage below.

I'm supposed to go to drama group every Monday knight, but this weak I'm too tired. I've had a very busy day at school and I'm not feeling grate. Instead, I think I'm going to stay hear and watch a film that I haven't scene before.

2) Circle the correct homophone to complete each sentence below.
a) Make sure that you know *wear / where* you are going.
b) Watch out for the crab — it has very sharp *claws / clause*.
c) At the theme park, we *road / rode* on four different roller coasters.
d) The jockey pulled on the *reigns / reins* to get the horse to stop.

Practise putting homophones into sentences...

REVISION TIP Using a clock or watch, give yourself three minutes to make a list of as many homophones as you can think of. Then try putting all the words you came up with into sentences.

Prefixes and Suffixes

Don't get your fixes in a twist — revise how to use prefixes and suffixes for the test...

Prefixes go at the Start of Words

Remember — 'pre' = 'before', so prefixes always go at the start of words.

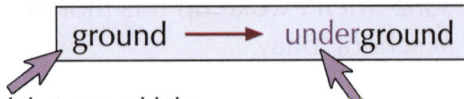

1) Add a prefix at the start of a word to make a new word.

ground → underground		clockwise → anticlockwise

The word that you add the prefix to is called the root word.

'under' is the prefix

'anti' is the prefix

2) Here are some common prefixes and an example of a word that uses each one:

ex → exchange	mis → misbehave	sub → submarine
re → replay	non → nonsense	inter → interchange
de → defrost	pre → preheat	trans → transport
un → unhappy	dis → disadvantage	counter → counteract

Suffixes go at the End of Words

1) Add a suffix to the end of a word to make a new word.

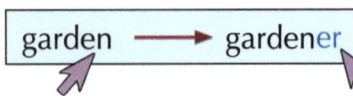

garden → gardener	turn → turning

'garden' is the root word.

'er' is the suffix

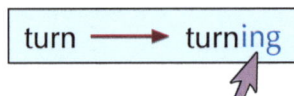

'ing' is the suffix

2) Here's a list of common suffixes with a word that uses each one:

s → chickens	ly → particularly	ness → sadness
ed → turned	ful → tearful	able → comfortable
en → wooden	est → greatest	ment → treatment
es → classes	ity → normality	ation → information

3) Sometimes adding a suffix can change the spelling of the word:

travel → traveller	stop → stopping	take → taking

Prefixes and Suffixes

You could be asked to write the **Correct Prefix** or **Suffix**

EXAMPLE: **Write the correct prefix or suffix to complete the words in the sentences.**

a) I asked the waiter for a ☐☐ fill of my soft drink.

b) It was ☐☐ fortunate that you missed the last train home.

c) The travell ☐☐☐ left the airport an hour late after their flight was delayed.

d) Angus is the tall ☐☐☐ boy in school.

Method — Read through each sentence carefully

1) You need to add a prefix to parts a) and b). Make sure that the prefix agrees with the meaning of the rest of the sentence.

a) I asked the waiter for a r e fill of my soft drink.

The speaker is asking for another drink.
The word is 'refill', so the correct prefix is 're'.

b) It was u n fortunate that you missed the last train home.

The sentence is talking about having bad luck,
so the correct prefix to add is 'un' to make 'unfortunate'.

2) Look at the whole sentence in parts c) and d) to help you choose the correct suffix.

c) The travell e r s left the airport an hour late after their flight was delayed.

You need to add a plural suffix here as the sentence talks about a group of people. Add 'ers' to make 'travellers'.

'their' usually tells you that it was more than one person.

d) Angus is the tall e s t boy in school.

The sentence is about the 'most tall' boy in school, so the correct suffix is 'est'.

Practice Questions

1) Complete the sentences by adding the correct prefix or suffix to the word in brackets.

a) The baby polar bear is so _____ (adore).

b) I was trying to be _____ (help) when I washed the dishes.

c) The ball hit Kayley and knocked her _____ (conscious).

d) Lyla's feeling of _____ (happy) increased when she found her shoes.

The spelling of the root word may change.

If you're stuck, try out different prefixes and suffixes...

REVISION TIP If you're struggling to think of the right prefix or suffix while you're revising, try saying some options out loud. 'Unfortunate' sounds just right, whereas 'disfortunate' doesn't.

Silent Letters and Double Letters

Silent letters and double letters in words can trip up even the most accomplished spellers.
There's a good chance that they'll come up in the test, so make sure you know them inside out...

Some words have **Silent Letters**

1) Some words are not spelt the way they sound. They have silent letters which you don't hear.
2) Here are some common examples:

Words with a Silent 'h'

| which | whistle | when |
| choir | chemist | rhino |

Words with a Silent 'k'

| knock | knife | knuckle |
| knight | know | knowledge |

Lots more words have silent letters — these are some of the common ones.

Words with a Silent 'b'

| comb | numb | debt |
| tomb | thumb | doubt |

Words with a Silent 'c'

| yacht | science | scissors |
| scent | rescind | descend |

Words with a Silent 'w'

| write | wrist | wrong |
| wrap | answer | who |

Words with a Silent 't'

| listen | whistle |
| thistle | castle |

Words with a Silent 'l'

| salmon | could |
| would | should |

Words with **Double Letters** can be **Tricky**

These words have double letters that you say as a single sound:

accommodation	appalling
address	association
aggressive	balloon
annual	coffee

committed	disappear
deterrent	embarrass
different	essential
dilemma	eventually

Think of ways to remember spellings you find tricky, e.g. 'necessary' could be: Never Eat Chips; Eat Salad Sandwiches And Remain Young.

exaggerate	jewellery
finally	necessary
immediately	occasion
irresistible	occurrence

parallel	spelling
possess	succeed
professor	success
recommend	tomorrow

Silent Letters and Double Letters

You may have to find **Words** that are **Spelt Wrong**

EXAMPLE: **Circle the spelling mistakes in the passage below.**

> 1   Tomorow morning I leave for an autum trip with my youth group. We woud
> 2   like to go to the Lake District as we usually do, but instead we're going to the
> 3   New Forest. We've got lots of fun acttivities planned like hiking and climing,
> 4   and every knight we will sit by the campfire and eat toasted marshmallows.

Method — Look for silent letters and double letters

1) Work carefully through the passage <u>one line</u> at a time.

2) Look for words that are <u>missing</u> a silent letter, or where double letters are used <u>incorrectly</u>.

> (Tomorrow) morning I leave for an (autumn) trip with my youth group. We (would)

'Tomorrow' has a double 'r'.   'autumn' has a silent 'n' at the end.   'would' has a silent 'l'.

> like to go to the Lake District as we usually do, but instead we're going to the

There are no spelling mistakes in this line.

> New Forest. We've got lots of fun (activities) planned like hiking and (climbing,)

A double 't' is not needed after 'c'. It should be spelt as 'activities'.   'climbing' has a silent 'b'.

> and every (night) we will sit by the campfire and eat toasted marshmallows.

This should be 'night'. It isn't spelt with a silent 'k' when it means the opposite of day.

The context of the sentence should give you clues about how to spell some words.

Practice Questions

1) Each sentence contains one spelling mistake. Rewrite the sentences, using the correct word.
   a) I maintainned a comfortable position for the whole journey.
   b) You need to wear more cloths in winter to keep warm.
   c) My interresting entry will win the competition tomorrow.

2) Rewrite the sentences, using the correct word.
   a) Everyone agreed that the charity event had been *successful / successfull / sucessful*.
   b) While we're in London, we want to visit Nelson's *Colum / Collumn / Column*.
   c) Sasha is the most *intelligent / inteligent / inteliggent* girl in the class.
   d) I arrived just as the show was *begining / beginning / beggining*.

Practise spelling any words you find hard to remember...

Some of these words are pretty tricky to spell, so write them out until they're fixed in your head.

Other Awkward Spellings

Bad news, I'm afraid — there are even more words that don't follow the rules. Some of them are pretty common too, so make sure you know how to spell them before you sit the test.

The 'i' before 'e' rule

1) Revise this rule — it's important:

> 'i' before 'e' except after 'c', but only when it rhymes with bee.

The whole word doesn't need to rhyme with bee, just the 'ie' sound.

2) Here are some examples:

bel**ie**ve

The 'ie' sound rhymes with bee, so 'i' goes before 'e'.

th**ie**f

rec**ei**ve

It rhymes with bee, and there's a 'c', so the 'i' goes after the 'e'.

sc**ie**nce

It's after 'c', but it doesn't rhyme with bee, so 'i' goes before 'e'.

n**ei**ghbour

It doesn't rhyme with bee, so it's 'ei' instead of 'ie'.

eight

It doesn't rhyme with bee, so 'e' goes before 'i'.

3) There are a few exceptions to the rule, like 'weird' and 'seize'.

Unstressed Vowels can make words tricky to spell

1) Sometimes the vowel sound in a word isn't clear — these sounds are called unstressed vowels.

2) Spelling these words can be awkward because the vowels don't make the sound you would expect.

Make up some short phrases to help you remember how to spell words with unstressed vowels, e.g. "I'm at a private party".

private

'private' sounds like it should be spelt 'privite'.

sep**a**rate

'separate' sounds like it should be spelt 'seperate'.

3) Unfortunately there isn't a rule for spelling words with unstressed vowels — so make sure you know how to spell them. Here are some examples:

defin**i**tely	doct**o**r	occurr**e**nce
r**i**diculous	diff**e**rence	comp**a**ny
governm**e**nt	anim**a**l	interfer**e**nce
gen**e**ral	bisc**u**it	carp**e**t
d**e**scribe	jewell**e**ry	miser**a**ble

Other Awkward Spellings

You may have to **Add Letters** to a **Word**

EXAMPLE: Fill in the missing letters to complete the words in the sentences below.

a) Adam was rel[ ][ ]ved to find his maths homework.

b) There are p[ ][ ]ces of broken glass everywhere.

c) The villain was very dec[ ][ ]tful.

d) I often w[ ][ ]gh my cat to make sure that she is healthy.

Method — Remember the 'i before e' rule

1) Work out the word that is being added to each sentence.

2) Think carefully about the spelling — look at the letters before and after the gap.

a) Adam was rel(i)(e)ved to find his maths homework.

The letter before the gap is 'l' and the 'ie' sound in 'relieved' rhymes with bee.

So 'ie' is the correct spelling to use.

b) There are p(i)(e)ces of broken glass everywhere.

The letter before the gap is 'p' and the 'ie' sound rhymes with bee.

So 'pieces' should be spelt with an 'ie'.

Don't get confused by the 'c' after the gap — it doesn't matter which letter comes after the 'ie' sound.

c) The villain was very dec(e)(i)tful.

The letter before the gap is 'c' and the 'ie' sound rhymes with bee.

This time you need to add 'ei' to spell 'deceitful'.

d) I often w(e)(i)gh my cat to make sure that she is healthy.

The letter before the gap is 'w', but the 'ie' sound does not rhyme with bee.

You should add 'ei' to spell 'weigh'.

Practice Questions

1) Circle the correctly spelt word to complete the sentences below.

a) My car is running out of *diesel / deisel*.
b) Zaneb went to the museum to see the *ancient / anceint* remains.

2) The words below are missing unstressed vowels. Write the correct vowel in each gap.

a) desp[ ]rate   b) fact[ ]ry   c) respons[ ]ble   d) lit[ ]r[ ]ture

REVISION TIP

Don't let awkward spellings catch you out...

If you keep spelling a word incorrectly while you're revising, write it on a sticky note and put it somewhere you'll see it every day. This will help the right spelling stick in your mind.

Practice Questions

You've almost finished the Spelling section. All that's left now is to test your knowledge with these practice questions. If you get any wrong, don't worry — recap the rules and have another go.

Plurals

> Write the correct plural of the word in brackets. Look at this example:
>
> **Example:** Overhead, we saw dozens of ___meteors___ (meteor).

1. During the drive, I kept seeing _____ (**flash**) of light in the distance.

2. Lola was presented with a variety of _____ (**cheese**).

3. My mobile phone number has six _____ (**zero**) in it.

4. The artist exhibited her _____ (**sketch**) of the coastline.

5. Annie and Ted had different _____ (**logo**) on their school uniforms.

> Underline the correct plural to complete the sentence. Look at this example:
>
> **Example:** I filled my new (**shelfs** **shelves** **shelfes**) with books.

6. We kept all of the sweets to (**ourselfs** **ourself** **ourselves**).

7. The final two (**series** **serieses** **seriess**) of *Space Voyage* were incredible.

8. Long ago, (**cavemens** **cavemen** **cavemans**) hunted for woolly mammoths.

9. I like to have (**cherrys** **cherryies** **cherries**) on top of my ice cream.

10. Rabbits tend to produce a lot of (**offsprings** **offspring** **offspringes**).

Practice Questions

Homophones

> Choose the correct homophone from the brackets. Look at this example.
>
> **Example:** The lizard basked in the sun's _____*rays*_____ (rays raise).

11. Eli finally realised he'd been waiting in the wrong _____ (cue queue).

12. The jail in the dungeon had _____ (barred bard) windows.

13. Lina was incredibly composed — nothing _____ (fazed phased) her.

14. The climber pulled on the rope until it was _____ (taut taught).

15. A cold _____ (draft draught) was coming from Elliot's window.

> Underline the correct homophone to complete the sentence. Look at this example.
>
> **Example:** I'm too busy to chat (write rite <u>right</u>) now.

16. Jess couldn't row because she'd dropped an **(or ore oar)** into the water.

17. The thief was told to **(seize seas sees)** the jewels.

18. The leopard **(prays preys praise)** upon mammals, birds and fish.

19. Someone **(wrapped rapt rapped)** on my door while I was trying to sleep.

20. Maya **(piqued peaked peeked)** through the gap in the curtains.

Practice Questions

Prefixes and Suffixes

> Choose the correct prefix from the list to complete the word in each sentence: **un**, **in**, **pre**, **mis**, **re** or **dis**. Look at this example:
>
> **Example:** His superpower made him __in__ visible.

21. In his hurry to get to the airport, Dylan _____placed his passport.

22. The doctor had to _____scribe new medication for three of her patients.

23. Her boisterous nephews and nieces left the house in a state of _____order.

24. Mei wore large sunglasses, hoping to remain _____recognisable.

25. For the sixth time that day, Afzal had to _____adjust his tie.

> Complete these sentences by adding a suffix to the word in brackets. Look at this example:
>
> **Example:** The tightrope walker was very ___careful___ (care).

26. The troublesome meerkats needed constant _____ (**supervise**).

27. Ruby gasped when she spotted _____ (**move**) in the shadows.

28. Golden retrievers are very _____ (**rely**) companions.

29. The remote island was famous for its _____ (**tranquil**).

30. Ava took _____ (**owner**) of planning the surprise party.

Practice Questions

Silent Letters

Each sentence contains a spelling mistake. Underline the word with the error and write the correct spelling on the line. Look at this example:

Example: Anna dipped her <u>thum</u> in paint. ___*thumb*___

31. There was no dout that Johnny had stolen the biscuits. _____

32. My aim is to eventually aquire a large fortune. _____

33. When I'm running, I breath very loudly. _____

34. The snake rithed when the hunter picked it up. _____

35. The calm lake glisened in the moonlight. _____

Double Letters

Underline the correct word to complete each sentence. Look at this example:

Example: I built a tower out of cake, but it (**topled** <u>**toppled**</u> **toplled**) over.

36. We were (**forbiden   forbbiden   forbidden**) from entering the attic.

37. Mo (**assummed   asumed   assumed**) that the weather would stay nice.

38. Rose thought that buying three bikes was a bit (**exccessive   excessive   exccesive**).

39. All the twists and turns in the maze left him (**beefuddled   beffuddled   befuddled**).

40. The general (**sumoned   summoned   summonned**) all of his soldiers.

Practice Questions

Awkward Spellings

> Add either **ie** or **ei** to form the words correctly. Look at this example:
>
> **Example:** The horses pulled the sl_ei_gh through the snow.

41. The goalkeeper was sent to retr____ve the ball from the back of the net.

42. Sebastian politely f____gned interest in the boring conversation.

43. Jackson's new kitten was rather misch____vous.

44. Often, my parents and I go for a l____surely stroll after dinner.

45. Ellie's consc____nce impelled her to help the animals.

> Underline the correct spelling to complete each sentence. Look at this example:
>
> **Example:** When Lucy lost her toy, she was (**miserable** misarable).

46. Bai wrote a beautiful (**description** **discription**) of his garden.

47. I like pasta, but pizza would always be my (**preferance** **preference**).

48. She received a (**handsome** **hansome**) reward for catching the thief.

49. The two violinists played in perfect (**harmeny** **harmony**) with each other.

50. Zara's pirate party was a (**memorable** **memorible**) event.

Practice Questions

Mixed Spelling Questions

Underline the correct word to complete each sentence. Look at this example:

Example: Joe has a **(flare <u>flair</u>)** for making sculptures out of sand.

51. Lilly was unsure whether to **(brooch   broach)** the topic.

52. The collection of **(scarfs   scarves)** belongs to Pascal.

53. My physics teacher was **(formerly   formally)** a firefighter.

54. I used to think that thunderstorms were **(frightning   frightening)**.

55. To spot owls at night, you have to be **(observant   observent)**.

Each sentence contains a spelling mistake. Underline the word with the error and write the correct spelling on the line. Look at this example:

Example: I like reading poems with lots of <u>rimes</u>.   <u>rhymes</u>

56. Fred frequently wore colourful accesories.   _____

57. The hungry lion bared its teeth in a show of agression.   _____

58. The ancient oak tree had a narled trunk.   _____

59. The final asent to the top of the mountain was exhausting.   _____

60. Nina gave us a sutle clue to where the treasure was buried.   _____

Preparing for Word Meaning Questions

Thankfully, reading the dictionary isn't the only thing that'll help you pass the VR part of the test...

Practise spotting different Word Types

1) 'Word type' means what category a word belongs to — e.g. noun, verb, adjective or adverb.
2) Here are a few tips to help you work out word types:

Nouns are people, places or things

1) Concrete nouns are objects and things.

> cow   apple   dog   milk

2) Abstract nouns are harder to spot — they're things you can't see, hear, taste, touch or smell.

> childhood   freedom   bravery   adventure

3) Proper nouns are the names of particular people, places or things.

> Heather is going to Rome in July.   ← Proper nouns always start with a capital letter.

Verbs describe actions

1) A verb can be a doing word like 'dance', or a being word like 'is'.
2) Verbs can go after 'I', 'you', 'he', 'it', 'she' or 'they'.

> I play, you dance, they are, it was

> Some words belong to more than one word type. E.g. 'I catch fish', 'There's a catch'. 'Catch' is a verb in the first sentence and a noun in the other.

Adverbs describe verbs

1) Adverbs add extra information — they tell you how, when, where or why an action is done.
2) Adverbs often end in -ly.

> quickly, happily, playfully

Adjectives describe nouns

Adjectives sometimes end with -y, -ly, -ing, -ous, -ful or -able.

> sandy, friendly, interesting, gorgeous, peaceful, comfortable

---

REVISION TIP

Get comfortable with word types...

The next time you open a book, pick a few sentences at random and see how quickly you can identify all the different nouns, verbs, adverbs and adjectives in those sentences.

Preparing for Word Meaning Questions

Use **Word Type** to work out the **Answer**

Recognising word types can be a useful way of solving some questions in the VR part of your 11+ test.

Put a word in a sentence to work out its **Word Type**

Sometimes a word may belong to more than one word type so you might be able to use it in a few different ways:

> Being able to work out word type can help you if you don't know what a word means.

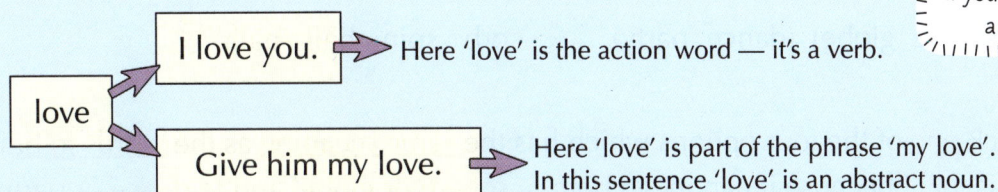

love
→ I love you. → Here 'love' is the action word — it's a verb.
→ Give him my love. → Here 'love' is part of the phrase 'my love'. In this sentence 'love' is an abstract noun.

Look at word endings to help you work out **Word Type**

1) Sometimes you might need to find words that mean the same thing.
2) If you don't recognise some of the words, you could try looking at word type to help you.

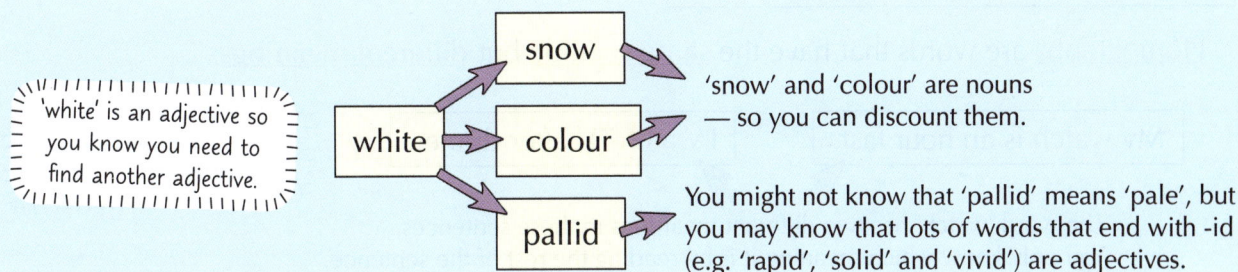

> 'white' is an adjective so you know you need to find another adjective.

white
→ snow
→ colour
→ pallid

'snow' and 'colour' are nouns — so you can discount them.

You might not know that 'pallid' means 'pale', but you may know that lots of words that end with -id (e.g. 'rapid', 'solid' and 'vivid') are adjectives.

Practice Questions

1) Work out the word type of each of the following words:
   a) sang   c) nosy   e) cryptic   g) vacantly
   b) honesty   d) tighten   f) play   h) talent

2) Write down the meaning and word type of the following words.
   a) truth   b) cantankerous   c) wrathfully   d) bemusement

> Check your answers in a dictionary.

There might be some words in the test that you don't know...

TEST TIP You'll recognise a lot of the words in the test, but there might be some tricky words in there to challenge you. If you come across a word you don't know, don't worry — try to eliminate as many of the other possible answers as you can, then make a sensible guess.

Multiple Meanings

These questions are on homographs — that's 'a word with more than one meaning' to you and me.

11+ Example Question

Take a look at this 11+ sample question:

> **EXAMPLE:** **Choose the word that has a similar meaning to the words in both sets of brackets.**
>
> (sphere globe) (dance party)   orb spin ball gala

- You need to pick one of the four options which has the same meaning as the words in brackets.
- So the answer is 'ball' because it can mean both 'a sphere or globe' and 'a dance or party'.

You need to be able to recognise Homographs for this question

Homographs have the Same Spelling

Homographs are words that have the same spelling but different meanings:

My watch is an hour fast.   I watch TV after dinner.

Homographs often belong to different word types.

The word 'watch' has two different meanings in these sentences.
You only know which meaning it is by reading the rest of the sentence.

Some homographs are Pronounced Differently

Some homographs have the same spelling, but are pronounced differently:

A female pig is a sow.   The farmer was going to sow her seeds.

The word 'sow' has two different meanings in these sentences.
They're also pronounced differently, but they're both spelt the same.

REVISION TIP

Think about words from different angles...

If you're stuck on a Multiple Meanings question when you're revising, try writing as many sentences as you can using the words in brackets. Think about whether each word can be used as a noun, verb, adjective or adverb, or as more than one of these word types.

Section Two — Word Meanings

Multiple Meanings

Work through each word One By One

EXAMPLE: Choose the word that has a similar meaning to the words in both sets of brackets.

(greet salute) (sleet snow)   wave rain hail storm

Method — Rule out the wrong options

1) <u>Read</u> through the words in the <u>brackets</u>.

2) Think about what both sets <u>mean</u>.

> You might not recognise one of the words in brackets, but the other one will mean the same thing. Work with the word you do know.

(greet salute) (sleet snow)   wave rain hail storm

'greet' and 'salute' mean 'to address someone'.

'sleet' and 'snow' are types of wet weather.

3) Take a look at the four options and try to <u>rule out</u> any possible answers.

'wave' can be a way of addressing someone, but it doesn't relate to wet weather — you can ignore it.

~~wave~~ rain hail storm

~~wave~~ ~~rain~~ (hail) ~~storm~~

> It might help to put a light pencil mark through any answers you've ruled out.

'rain' and 'storm' are types of wet weather, but they don't mean 'to address or salute'. That leaves us with 'hail'.

4) <u>Check</u> your answer by using the word in <u>two sentences</u> — one for <u>each meaning</u>.

The weather forecast predicted hail. ✓   All hail the new king. ✓

Practice Questions

Choose the word that has a similar meaning to the words in both sets of brackets.

1) (lecture discussion) (chat natter)   speak   talk   speech   articulate

2) (manage supervise) (sprint dash)   boss   rush   run   oversee

3) (schedule reserve) (novel text)   story   book   arrange   manual

TEST TIP

Try to give an answer for every question...

If you've narrowed down the options but you've still got more than one possible answer left, don't just leave the answer blank — a sensible guess is better than no answer at all.

Closest Meaning

This question type is about synonyms — that's another way of saying 'words with similar meanings'.

11+ Example Question

Here's an example of the sort of question you might get in the test:

> **EXAMPLE:** **Find the word that means the same, or nearly the same, as the word on the left.**
>
> **stroll**   march   delay   amble   stride

- You need to pick the word that has the closest meaning to the word on the left.
- The answer to this question is 'amble' — like 'stroll', it means 'to walk slowly'.

You need to know about Synonyms to answer these questions

1) Words with similar meanings are synonyms — e.g. 'small' and 'tiny'.
2) Pairs of synonyms are usually the same word type — e.g. nouns, verbs, adjectives or adverbs.

Some questions will try to Catch You Out

Make sure you pick the pair of words that mean the same thing — don't just pick two words that are connected.

bucket	spade (pail) barrel cauldron

You might pick 'spade' — although it's connected to 'bucket', it doesn't mean the same thing. The right answer is 'pail'.

write	paint paper read (scrawl)

You might have heard 'read' and 'write' used together, but they don't mean the same thing. The right answer is 'scrawl'.

lightly	(faintly) vaguely nervously brightly

'Light' and 'bright' can mean the same thing, but 'lightly' doesn't mean the same as 'brightly'. The right answer is 'faintly'.

> It may help you to picture the meaning of the words in your head so you can pick the pair that are the closest in meaning.

REVISION TIP

Double check your answers if you need to...

If you want to make sure you've got the right answer, try making up a sentence using the word on the left, then substitute in your answer. If the sentence means the same thing, it's the right answer. If it changes the meaning or doesn't make sense, try another word.

Closest Meaning

Use **Definitions** to help you answer the question

EXAMPLE: **Find the word that means the same, or nearly the same, as the word on the left.**

stick   fused   tree   install   club

Method 1 — Compare the meanings of words

1) Take the first word and think about its meaning.

| **stick** | → 'stick' means 'to glue something together' or 'a piece of wood'. |

'stick' can be a noun or a verb. Remember to think about different word types in the test.

2) Compare its meaning with each of the words on the right.

| fused | → 'fused' means 'joined together' or 'fitted with a fuse'. |

The first meaning of 'fused' is about joining things together, just like 'stick'. But it's in the past tense, whereas 'stick' is in the present tense. So they don't really mean the same thing.

| tree | → 'tree' means 'a large plant with a woody stem'. |

A stick comes from a tree, but they're not the same thing, so this isn't the answer.

| install | → 'install' means 'to put something in position and connect for use'. |

'Install' is about positioning something, not gluing it, so this isn't right either.

| club | → 'club' means 'a group of people with similar interests', 'a heavy piece of wood' or 'to hit someone with a stick'. |

This definition is similar to something we've seen before...

| **stick** | → 'stick' means 'to glue something together' or 'a piece of wood'. |

In the test, remember to compare all the words to make sure you've found the closest match.

3) 'stick' and 'club' are very close in meaning — so this is the answer.

Think about the possible meanings of a word first...

In this question, because 'fused' is the first option, you might automatically think of the verb definition of 'stick' rather than its other possible meanings. This is why it's a good idea to think about alternative definitions of the word on the left before you start going through the options.

Closest Meaning

You can also look at Word Type

EXAMPLE: **Find the word that means the same, or nearly the same, as the word on the left.**

rapidly   hasty   immediate   quickly   expeditious

Method 2 — Compare the word type

1) The correct answer will often be the <u>same type of word</u> as the word on the left — they'll both be nouns, verbs etc. — as well as having the <u>same meaning</u>.

Take a look back at p.22 if you're not sure about word type.

2) Start by looking at <u>word meaning</u> and <u>rule out</u> any words that don't mean the same thing.

| **rapidly** | hasty | ~~immediate~~ | quickly | expeditious |

You can rule out 'immediate' because it means 'this moment', which is different from 'rapidly'. You might not know what 'expeditious' means, but don't panic — you can still work out the answer.

3) Take each word and <u>use it in a sentence</u> to help you work out the word type.

He ate his dinner rapidly. ✓
He ate his dinner quickly. ✓

'rapidly' and 'quickly' both end in -ly and can be used in the same way. They're the same word type — adverbs.

He ate his dinner hasty. ✗

'hasty' can't be used in the same way as 'rapidly'. It also ends in -y, which helps you to work out that it's an adjective.

He ate his dinner expeditious. ✗

'expeditious' ends in -ous. Lots of adjectives end with -ous — vicious, dangerous, cautious — so 'expeditious' is probably an adjective.

4) By looking at the <u>meaning</u> and the <u>word type</u>, you can work out that '<u>quickly</u>' has the <u>closest meaning</u> to '<u>rapidly</u>'.

There's Another Type of synonym question you might get

Here's an <u>example</u> of the sort of question you might get in the <u>test</u>:

EXAMPLE: **Complete the word on the right so that it means the same as the word on the left.**

sea   o □ □ □ n

If you get stuck, use a thesaurus to help you with these questions.

- You need to think of a word that means the <u>same</u> as the word you're given, then write the <u>missing letters</u> in the boxes.
- A word that means the same as '<u>sea</u>' is '<u>ocean</u>', so the missing letters are '<u>c</u>', '<u>e</u>' and '<u>a</u>'.

Section Two — Word Meanings

Closest Meaning

EXAMPLE: **Complete the word on the right so that it means the same as the word on the left.**

test ⬚h⬚c⬚

Method — Use your knowledge of spelling patterns

1) If you can't spot the answer straight away, look at the letters you're <u>given</u> and see if you can spot any likely <u>spelling patterns</u>.

⬚h⬚c⬚ → The second letter is 'h'. At the start of a word, 'ch', 'sh' and 'th' are all common letter patterns.

There's just one letter missing between 'h' and 'c'. These are both consonants, so it's probably a vowel. ← ⬚h⬚c⬚

⬚h⬚c⬚ → The second to last letter is 'c'. At the end of a word, 'ce', 'ch' and 'ck' are all common letter patterns.

2) Scribble down some words that <u>match</u> your <u>spelling patterns</u>. Think about whether any of them mean the same as the word you've been given.

thick shock shack chuck (check) → None of the others are close, but 'check' seems like it might work.

3) Try using the two words in the <u>same sentence</u> to make sure.

The doctor had to **test** my heart rate.

The doctor had to **check** my heart rate. → The two words can be used in the same way, so 'check' is the answer.

Practice Questions

1) Find the word that means the same, or nearly the same, as the word on the left.

   a) **afraid**   aghast   shocked   petrified   cowardly
   b) **trail**   traipse stride   track   tread
   c) **smiled**   sneered grimaced   chuckled   beamed

2) Complete the word on the right so it means the same as the word on the left.

   a) **light** ⬚l⬚⬚⬚   b) **story** ⬚⬚⬚l⬚e   c) **jump** ⬚⬚⬚e⬚a

TEST TIP

Always read the question wording really carefully...

In the test, you could also be asked to find words with **opposite** meanings (p. 30-33). These questions will be in the same format as Closest Meaning questions, so be sure to read the instructions carefully to make sure you answer the question in the right way.

Opposite Meaning

The opposite of good is bad. The opposite of night is day. The opposite of synonym is antonym.

11+ Example Question

Here's an example of the sort of question you might get in the real thing:

If you can't spot the answer straight away, start by eliminating the words that are definitely wrong.

EXAMPLE: **Find the word that means the opposite, or nearly the opposite, of the word on the left.**

clean   untidy   squalid   dreary   sterile

- Pick the word that is most opposite in meaning to the word on the left.
- The answer is 'squalid' because it means 'dirty', which is the opposite of 'clean'.

This question is asking about Antonyms

1) Words that have opposite meanings are called antonyms — e.g. 'new' and 'old'.
2) Here are some more examples of antonyms:

fat	skinny, slender, slim, thin
shout	mumble, murmur, mutter, whisper
frail	strong, robust, sturdy, tough
accept	deny, decline, reject, spurn

Sets of antonyms will often be the same word type.

Look at the Prefixes

You can turn some words into antonyms by adding certain prefixes such as un-, dis- or in-.

lock, tidy, friendly, well	unlock, untidy, unfriendly, unwell
appear, please, like, agree	disappear, displease, dislike, disagree
direct, edible, formal, active	indirect, inedible, informal, inactive

Practice makes perfect... inaction makes imperfect...

REVISION TIP

If you want to practise thinking of antonyms, open your favourite book and choose a paragraph. Read through the paragraph, writing down all of the verbs, adjectives and adverbs that you find. Then, jot down as many antonyms as you can think of for each one.

Opposite Meaning

Use **Definitions** to help you answer the question

EXAMPLE: **Find the word that means the opposite, or nearly the opposite, of the word on the left.**

frequently   seldom   constantly   uncommon   sometimes

Method 1 — Compare the meanings of words

You can use a similar method for the opposite and closest meanings questions.

1) Take the <u>word</u> on the <u>left</u> and think about its <u>meaning</u>.

| (frequently)   seldom   constantly   uncommon   sometimes |

'frequently' means 'often'.

2) Compare its <u>meaning</u> with each word on the <u>right</u>.

| seldom | → | 'seldom' means 'hardly ever'. |

| constantly | → | 'constantly' means 'continuing without pause'. |

| uncommon | → | 'uncommon' means 'unusual'. |

| sometimes | → | 'sometimes' means 'every now and then'. |

In the exam, remember to compare all the words, to make sure you've found the words with the most opposite meaning.

3) '<u>frequently</u>' means 'often', whereas '<u>seldom</u>' means 'hardly ever', so these are the <u>most opposite</u> in meaning.

4) If you have time, think of a <u>sentence</u> which uses the <u>first word</u>. Then try swapping in the <u>second word</u> to see if it makes the sentence mean the <u>opposite</u>.

| I frequently swim before school. |

| I seldom swim before school. |

The first sentence means the opposite of the second, so 'seldom' is definitely the right answer.

Try putting the words into a sentence...

REVISION TIP

Sometimes there might be another word that seems like a possible answer, for example, 'uncommon' in the question above. This is where using the words in a sentence can help — 'I uncommon swim before school' doesn't make sense, so this can't be your answer.

Opposite Meaning

Use **Word Type** to find the answer

EXAMPLE: Find the word that means the opposite, or nearly the opposite, of the word on the left.

contract   disputed dwindle dilate expansion

Method 2 — Compare the word type

1) <u>Read</u> the question. <u>Think</u> about the meaning of the word on the left.

> **contract** → 'contract' can be a <u>noun</u> meaning 'a written or spoken agreement'. It can also be a <u>verb</u> meaning 'to shrink' or 'to catch a disease'.

2) Now <u>look</u> at the options and see if you can <u>rule any out</u> based on what they <u>mean</u>.

> disputed → 'disputed' means 'disagreed' — this is the opposite of 'agreement', so this could be the answer.

> ~~dwindle~~ → 'dwindle' means 'shrink'. This is the <u>same</u> as one of the meanings of 'contract', so we can rule this one out.

> dilate → 'dilate' means 'expand' — this is the opposite of 'shrink', so this could be the answer.

> expansion → 'expansion' means 'growth' — this is the opposite of 'shrink', so this could be the answer.

3) Once you've <u>narrowed down</u> your options, think about the <u>word type</u> of the remaining words. The answer will often be the <u>same word type</u> as the word on the left.

4) Take each word and work out its <u>word type</u>.

> ~~disputed~~ → 'disputed' is a <u>verb</u> or an <u>adjective</u>. The meaning of 'contract' that relates to agreement is a <u>noun</u>, so this <u>can't</u> be the answer.

> dilate → 'dilate' is a <u>verb</u>. The meaning of contract that relates to shrinking is also a <u>verb</u>. This looks like a likely answer.

Try using the word in a sentence to help you work out its word type.

> ~~expansion~~ → 'expansion' is a <u>noun</u>. The meaning of contract that relates to shrinking is a <u>verb</u>, so this can't be the answer.

5) By looking at the <u>meaning</u> and the <u>word type</u>, you can work out that '<u>dilate</u>' is the <u>most opposite</u> in meaning to 'contract'.

REVISION TIP

Don't forget words can have more than one meaning...

Some words belong to more than one word type, so think about the different meanings of words. For example, the noun 'fly' refers to an insect, but the verb can mean 'to soar'.

Opposite Meaning

You might also have to Fill in the Gaps in a word

EXAMPLE: Complete the word on the right so that it means the opposite of the word on the left.

best ☐ ☐ r s ☐

Method — Check your answer carefully

1) Often, the answer to these questions will jump out at you. It's tempting to race through them, but if you're not careful you could lose marks.

2) Before you write in your answer, check that you've read the question properly.

best f i r s t ✗ → It's easy to misread the question and write in a word that means the same, rather than the opposite.

3) Make sure you read the word you're given carefully too.

best w o r s e ✗ → This answer is nearly right, but 'best' means 'most good', so you need a word that means 'most bad'. Check your answer by writing the given word in a sentence, and then trying your options in the same sentence.

It was the best day ever. → It was the worse day ever. ✗
→ It was the worst day ever. ✓

The first sentence doesn't make sense, but the second one does, so 'worst' is your answer.

4) Check your spelling carefully, to make sure you haven't made any silly mistakes. If you're not sure of a spelling, writing it out a few different ways can help — sometimes one way will just look right.

wurst ✗
werst ✗
worst ✓

Practice Questions

1) Find the word that means the opposite, or nearly the opposite, of the word on the left.
   a) **present**   vacant   available   absent   blank
   b) **accuse**   preserve   defend   protect   shelter

2) Complete the word on the right so it means the opposite of the word on the left.
   a) **early** l☐☐☐☐   b) **wrong** ☐i☐☐t   c) **hard** ☐☐☐☐t

TEST TIP **Use your word making skills to help you find the answer...**
Don't worry if the answer doesn't jump out at you right away. Use your knowledge of prefixes, suffixes and other letter combinations to work out how to complete a word.

Odd One Out

The best way to revise for Odd One Out questions is to make sure your vocabulary is top-notch...

11+ Example Question

Here's an example of the sort of question you might get in the test:

> **EXAMPLE:** **Three of the words in the list are linked. Mark the word that is not related to these three.**
>
> whisper   bellow   murmur   mutter

- You need to pick one of the four words that isn't connected to the other three.
- The answer is 'bellow' because the rest of the words describe speaking quietly.

Use Word Meaning to find the answer

> **EXAMPLE:** **Three of the words in the list are linked. Mark the word that is not related to these three.**
>
> steal   borrow   lend   snatch

Method 1 — Compare the meanings of words

1) Read through all the words. Think about what each word means.

   steal → 'steal' means 'to take something without permission'.

   borrow → 'borrow' means 'to take something temporarily'.

   lend → 'lend' means 'to give something temporarily'.

   snatch → 'snatch' means 'to take something suddenly'.

   This question is testing your knowledge of word meanings.

2) Try to make a connection between three of the words.

   The odd one out won't always be the opposite of the other three — it just has to be unrelated to them.

   ~~steal~~   ~~borrow~~   (lend)   ~~snatch~~

   'steal', 'borrow' and 'snatch' all mean 'to take' — 'lend' means 'to give'.

3) The odd one out is 'lend' — so that's your answer.

Odd One Out

Use **Word Type** to find the answer

EXAMPLE: Three of the words in the list are linked. Mark the word that is not related to these three.

blemish   error   stain   mark

Method 2 — Compare the word type

1) Sometimes you might get a list of words that have <u>similar meanings</u>. To solve these questions it might help to think about <u>word type</u>.

2) <u>Read</u> through all the words. Think about the <u>word type</u> of each word.

blemish   error   stain   mark
noun verb   noun   noun verb   noun verb

Remember some words belong to more than one word type.

3) <u>Identify</u> any word types that <u>don't match</u> the others. Here, all four words can be <u>nouns</u> and three can be <u>verbs</u>.

4) It looks like '<u>error</u>' could be the odd one out, but have a think about what the words <u>mean</u> to make sure.

blemish   error   stain

'Blemish' and 'stain' both mean 'an imperfection' or 'to make an imperfection'. 'Error' means 'something misguided or incorrect'.

'Mark' can mean 'a score' or 'to give a score', but it can also mean 'an imperfection' or 'to make an imperfection'.

blemish   stain   mark

5) 'Blemish', 'stain' and 'mark' are <u>synonyms</u>, so '<u>error</u>' is the <u>odd one out</u>.

Practice Questions

Three of the words in each list are linked. Mark the word that is not related to these three.

1) peaceful   dull   dreary   tedious
2) biography   recipe   newspaper   novel
3) lethargic   drowsy   listless   dormant
4) cheerful   morose   exultant   ecstatic

Make sure you know your nouns...

REVISION TIP If you're given a group of four nouns and you are struggling to work out which one is the odd one out, try thinking about the nature or purpose of the object or thing that each noun refers to. It'll help you to spot the one that doesn't fit with the others.

Reorder Words to Make a Sentence

Reorder the sentence in this words and halfway you're there...

11+ Example Question

Here's an <u>example</u> of the sort of question you might be asked in the test:

EXAMPLE: **The words below can be rearranged to form a sentence. Mark the word that doesn't fit in the sentence.**

watchings whole through film slept grandad the

- You need to <u>rearrange</u> the words to make a <u>sentence</u> that makes sense. You should have one word <u>left over</u> — you need to mark this <u>word</u>.
- The <u>answer</u> to this question is '<u>watchings</u>' — the <u>sentence</u> is: 'Grandad slept through the whole film.'

Try building a **Simple Sentence** first

EXAMPLE: **The words below can be rearranged to form a sentence. Mark the word that doesn't fit in the sentence.**

the dinner burned microwave old heat my

Method 1 — Make a basic sentence

1) Make a <u>complete sentence</u> using as <u>few</u> of the words as you can.

the microwave burned ← This is a good start, but there are still quite a few words left.

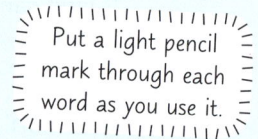

Put a light pencil mark through each word as you use it.

2) Try <u>extending</u> the sentence so it uses more words. You might need to <u>rearrange</u> it.

the microwave burned my dinner ← This uses most of the words. There are just two left — 'old' and 'heat'.

3) Try to fit one of the <u>remaining words</u> into your sentence.

old the microwave burned my dinner

the old microwave burned my dinner

The first sentence doesn't work, but the second one does. This is your sentence.

4) Check to see which word you <u>haven't used</u> in the sentence.

'heat' is the only word that hasn't been used, so this is your answer. → the dinner burned microwave old (heat) my

Reorder Words to Make a Sentence

You can also look at **Sentence Structure**

EXAMPLE: **The words below can be rearranged to form a sentence. Mark the word that doesn't fit in the sentence.**

among under troll scowled sat the and bridge the

Have a look at pages 46-49 for more on how to structure sentences.

Method 2 — Think about how sentences are formed

1) Look at the words. Sentences often start with a <u>subject</u> (i.e. the person or thing <u>doing the action</u> in the sentence). This is usually a <u>noun</u> or <u>pronoun</u> (e.g. 'I', 'he', 'she').

among under (troll) scowled sat the and (bridge) the → There are two nouns here, and no pronouns. Try the first noun as the start of your sentence.

the troll → 'troll' needs an article like 'a' or 'the' in front of it.

2) The subject is usually <u>followed</u> by a <u>verb</u>. There are two here — 'scowled' and 'sat'. → the troll scowled / sat

3) The next bit of the sentence might tell us <u>where</u> the troll is sitting or scowling, so look for words that are about <u>place</u>. → the troll scowled / sat among / under the bridge

The word 'bridge' is there, so that must be where the troll is. There are two words that relate to position — 'among' and 'under', so you need to decide which is correct.

'under the bridge' makes more sense than 'among the bridge'. → the troll scowled / sat ~~among~~ / under the bridge

4) There aren't many words left, so they should <u>slot into place</u> easily.

the troll sat under the bridge and scowled ← This sentence seems to make the most sense.

5) The only word we haven't used is '<u>among</u>', so that's the <u>answer</u>.

Practice Questions

The words below can be rearranged to form a sentence.
Mark the word that doesn't fit in the sentence.

1) girl know is are the I happiest Jo

2) caught walrus the into sea the and a fish rock dived

3) the if want field to quickly get there footpath take you

REVISION TIP

Read, read and read some more...

It'll really help you in the test if you're familiar with how sentences are constructed — reading lots of books, newspapers and magazines can help you build this understanding.

Practice Questions

That's nearly it for the Word Meanings section — now it's time to practise what you've learnt. If you're struggling with a question, have another look at the relevant page for that topic.

Multiple Meanings

Choose the word that has a similar meaning to the words in both sets of brackets. Underline your answer. Look at this example:

Example: (delicacy luxury) (cure heal)   treat aid delight care

1. **(institution academy)**   **(educate teach)**   school college learn class

2. **(question challenge)**   **(face tackle)**   ambush confront strike accost

3. **(hint suggestion)**   **(murmur mutter)**   sign mumble secret whisper

4. **(bright brilliant)**   **(kindle ignite)**   light intelligent glow shine

5. **(inconvenience trouble)** **(harass annoy)**   pest bother irk tease

6. **(obscured confused)**   **(murky overcast)**   muddled eclipsed clouded dim

7. **(lacking needing)**   **(lost mislaid)**   away deficient omitted missing

8. **(provide give)**   **(present submit)**   transfer offer afford gift

9. **(enclosure paddock)**   **(write compose)**   coop scribble pen compound

10. **(miracle marvel)**   **(awe amazement)**   oddity revere shock wonder

11. **(deserve warrant)**   **(virtue benefit)**   earn desire justify merit

12. **(stop halt)**   **(post deploy)**   station pause transmit appoint

Practice Questions

Closest Meaning

Find the word that means the same, or nearly the same, as the word on the left. Underline your answer. Look at this example:

Example: drab   pull loose harsh <u>dull</u>

13. **clasp**   tighten capture clutch loop

14. **relentless**   impatient relieved furious continuous

15. **counter**   oppose back brace deny

16. **style**   ability technique qualification process

17. **extent**   expand range border destination

18. **delay**   sedate abolish detain cancel

19. **crouch**   quiver stoop compress perch

20. **detailed**   exaggerated exhaustive copious precise

21. **particle**   dosage entity visible granule

22. **forward**   dominant gracious bold discourteous

23. **withdraw**   undertake invert bestow retract

24. **linger**   loiter prolong inhibit amble

Practice Questions

Complete the word on the right so that it means the same, or nearly the same, as the word on the left. Look at this example:

Example: sure ⎡c⎤ ⎡*e*⎤ ⎡r⎤ ⎡t⎤ ⎡*a*⎤ ⎡i⎤ ⎡n⎤

25. **judge** ⎡a⎤ ⎡s⎤ ⎡ ⎤ ⎡e⎤ ⎡ ⎤ ⎡ ⎤

26. **viewpoint** ⎡o⎤ ⎡ ⎤ ⎡ ⎤ ⎡l⎤ ⎡o⎤ ⎡ ⎤ ⎡k⎤

27. **tolerate** ⎡e⎤ ⎡ ⎤ ⎡d⎤ ⎡u⎤ ⎡ ⎤ ⎡ ⎤

28. **perforate** ⎡ ⎤ ⎡u⎤ ⎡ ⎤ ⎡c⎤ ⎡t⎤ ⎡ ⎤ ⎡r⎤ ⎡ ⎤

29. **unrest** ⎡ ⎤ ⎡u⎤ ⎡r⎤ ⎡ ⎤ ⎡ ⎤ ⎡i⎤ ⎡l⎤

Opposite Meaning

Find the word that means the opposite, or nearly the opposite, of the word on the left. Underline your answer. Look at this example:

Example: smooth   dirty <u>coarse</u> polished light

30. **expose**   deceive   review   uncover   conceal

31. **approach**   recede   proposal   evade   conclude

32. **conflict**   conserve   protect   discord   harmony

33. **unusual**   belated   unexpected   routine   mundane

Practice Questions

34. **flushed**   deserted   tarnished   ashen   serene

35. **overjoyed**   nonchalant   ecstatic   exasperated   devastated

36. **ally**   bystander   adversary   accomplice   guest

37. **inessential**   urgent   commanding   decisive   imperative

38. **uncommon**   prevalent   ruling   foreign   exceptional

39. **premature**   hasty   overdue   decrepit   foreseeable

40. **encourage**   disapprove   distrust   dispirit   disengage

41. **current**   impaired   obsolete   disregarded   exhausted

Complete the word on the right so that it means the opposite, or nearly the opposite, as the word on the left. Look at this example:

Example: honesty   d e c e i t

42. **extract**   i m [ ] l [ ] n [ ]

43. **secure**   u [ ] s [ ] [ ] b [ ] e

44. **liability**   a [ ] v a [ ] [ ] a [ ] e

45. **melodious**   [ ] u n [ ] l [ ] [ ] s

46. **unappreciative**   [ ] r [ ] t [ ] f [ ] l

Practice Questions

Odd One Out

Three of the words in each list are linked. Underline the word that is not related to these three. Look at this example:

Example: wind   gale   <u>shower</u>   hurricane

47. subordinate   chief   director   chairperson

48. jump   hurdle   rise   increase

49. lament   complain   mourn   grieve

50. affliction   disorder   therapy   condition

51. discipline   speciality   restraint   willpower

52. lump   morsel   slab   chunk

53. repel   repulse   defeat   disgust

54. futile   barren   ineffectual   fruitless

55. unspoken   hushed   wordless   mute

56. cut   slash   chafe   lacerate

57. expertise   proficiency   professional   prowess

58. concern   timidity   apprehension   uneasiness

Practice Questions

Reorder Words to Make a Sentence

Rearrange the words so that each sentence makes sense. Underline the word which doesn't fit into the sentence. Look at this example:

Example: waiter carried the dessert <u>tomorrow</u> the

59. astronaut the happily her moon inside floats spaceship

60. athletes run day trainer determined every miles the

61. a gave ribbon beautiful me bouquet she of flowers

62. going to am travel be world I the one day

63. my is part soldier in step-sister the a army

64. can Mateo Spanish and fluently speak English learned

65. motorway our repair down car broke rusty on the

66. holidaying skydiving are when in Thailand I went we were

67. scampered curious inside along the empty rat street the

68. has finished Penny novel will almost second writing her

69. is to tonight he bake chocolate icing planning a cake

70. Joe falls rock over tripped he when the protruding exclaimed

Preparing for Cloze Questions

'Cloze' tests are pieces of text with letters or words missing. You just have to fill in the missing bits...

You might have to **Choose** a **Whole Word**

1) In one type of cloze test, you're given some text with words missing. You have to choose the best word to fill each gap from three or four options.

2) Here's the type of passage you might get in the test:

EXAMPLE: **Choose the correct words to complete the passage.**

The answers on this page have already been filled in.

Polar bears live
☐ under
■ in
☐ with
the Arctic. They are the largest land

carnivores in the
☐ planet
☐ sea
■ world
and an adult male can weigh up to

700 kg. The number of polar bears has
■ declined
☐ decrease
☐ risen
in recent years

due to
■ hunting
☐ birth
☐ seals
and loss of sea ice.

You might have to **Fill In** missing **Letters**

1) In the second type of cloze test, you're given some text where some words have missing letters. You have to work out what the word should be, and write in the letters to complete it.

2) Here's the type of passage you might get in the test:

EXAMPLE: **Complete the text by filling in one missing letter per box.**

Bill Noggin was the ha[p][p][i][e]st fisherman in Cornwall. Every

morning at d[a][w]n he would pull on his gal[o][s][h]es, kiss his wife

goodbye and walk down to the quay, wh[i]st[l][i]ng a merry tune.

Everyone in the v[i][l][l]a[g]e knew Bill, and everyone liked him.

Everyone, that is, [e][x][c]ept for Regina Fillet, the butcher.

Preparing for Cloze Questions

Cloze Questions test your Vocabulary and English skills...

1) Cloze questions test your reading ability, vocabulary skills and knowledge of the rules of English.

2) In some types of cloze question, there'll often be more than one option that seems to work, but only one of them will be correct. Have a look at this question:

> The practice you've done for Word Meanings questions (see pages 22-37) will come in handy for Cloze questions too.

EXAMPLE:

The girls screamed ☐ noisy ☐ loudly ☐ strident when they saw the washing up.

3) All the options are related to noise, but only one — 'loudly' — is an adverb (a word that describes a verb, in this case 'screamed'). So this is the only one that works in the sentence.

4) You need to be able to form sentences that make sense and are grammatically correct, so you need to know the rules of English and grammar. These rules are covered on pages 46-49.

5) Do lots of writing practice to help you understand how sentences are formed — write letters and e-mails to friends and relatives, as well as stories or non-fiction texts about subjects that interest you.

They also test your Spelling

1) In other types of cloze question, good spelling is vital.

2) Have a look at the advice for improving your spelling on pages 4-15, and make sure you know your spelling patterns inside out.

Practice Questions

1) Circle the correct word to complete each sentence.
   a) It was getting *dark / sunny / quiet*, so I turned on the light.
   b) Stella fell off the camel and *jumped / crawled / landed* on her feet.
   c) Playing basketball *enlarges / accelerates / improves* your coordination.

2) Complete each sentence by filling in one missing letter per box.
   a) Chen and Beth ran away from the ☐☐ly monster.
   b) I go swimming with my ☐rie☐☐s every Monday night.
   c) My dog won't stop scratching — I think he has ☐l☐☐s.

Write your way to success...

REVISION TIP

You can practise your English skills by writing short stories, poems or even song lyrics. Have a go at using a thesaurus to make your vocabulary as interesting as possible.

Using Rules of English — Verbs

Having a good grasp of English rules and how sentences are put together will help with cloze questions. Luckily, the next few pages will help you recap all the important bits.

A **Sentence Always** has a **Verb**

> Verbs can also be 'being' words, e.g. in the sentence 'I am cold', the verb is 'am'.

1) Verbs are action words — they describe what the subject of the sentence is doing.

'Andy' is the subject because he is 'doing' the action. → Andy baked a cake. ← 'baked' is the verb.

Running is good for your health. ← 'Running' is the subject because the verb 'is' describes what the subject does.

2) The subject and verb have to agree. This just means that a singular subject needs a singular form of the verb, and a plural subject needs a plural form of the verb.

Majid is in the car.

Majid and Neha are in the car.

The subject is 'Majid'. It's singular, as there's only one person. The verb is 'is'. It's singular too. The subject here is 'Majid and Neha' — there's more than one person, so it's plural. The verb 'are' is also plural, to match the subject.

Phrases and **Clauses Add Information** to a **Sentence**

Phrases and clauses are groups of words that are used to form sentences.

A **Phrase Doesn't Normally** have a **Verb...**

A phrase doesn't usually contain a verb and it doesn't make sense on its own.

Jade wore her new purple dress. ← 'her new purple dress' is a noun phrase.

...But a **Clause Always Does**

Unlike a phrase, a clause always contains a verb.

Suzy listened to the radio while she brushed her teeth. ← This is a clause. The verb is 'brushed'.

The **Tense** of a verb tells you **When It's Happening**

Verbs can be in the past or the present tense. You can also use verbs to talk about things that will happen in the future.

Roberta played the lead role. ← past tense → Roberta has played the lead role.

Roberta plays the lead role. ← present tense → Roberta is playing the lead role.

Roberta will play the lead role. ← future → Roberta will be playing the lead role.

Sometimes there's more than one verb together in a sentence.

Using Rules of English — Verbs

Make sure that you can Use Verbs in the Correct Tense

EXAMPLE: In each sentence, one verb has been used incorrectly.
Rewrite the sentences using the correct form of the verb.

  a) "Quick, everyone went to your lookouts!" ordered the fireman.
  b) The ball was kick into the back of the net.
  c) My rabbit is escape at this very moment.
  d) Yesterday, my brother refuse to clean his bedroom.

Method — Work out when the action is happening

1) Read the first sentence and work out which verb is wrong.

   a) "Quick, everyone went to your lookouts!" ordered the fireman.

   This doesn't sound right. The fireman is issuing an instruction in the present tense, and 'went' is in the past tense.

   a) "Quick, everyone go to your lookouts!" ordered the fireman.

   This is better. The past tense 'went' has changed to the present tense, 'go'.

2) Do the same for the rest of the sentences:

   b) The ball was kicked into the back of the net.

   The clue here is 'was' — it tells you that the sentence is in the past tense. So you need to change 'kick' to 'kicked'.

   c) My rabbit is escaping at this very moment.

   'is' tells you that this sentence is in the present tense and it's still happening. So you need to change 'escape' to 'escaping'.

   d) Yesterday, my brother refused to clean his bedroom.

   The word 'Yesterday' tells you that the sentence is in the past tense. So use 'refused' instead of 'refuse'.

Practice Questions

1) Circle the correct verb to complete each sentence.
   a) Sadie has *eating / eat / eaten* all of my popcorn.
   b) I have *going / been / went* to South Africa on holiday.
   c) Barry's knee is *hurted / hurts / hurting* after he fell over.
   d) You should *got / go / went* home or you'll be late.
   e) What time do you think you will *arriving / arrive / arrived*?
   f) The dolphin is about to *leaps / leaping / leap* out of the water.

REVISION TIP

Use the whole sentence...

The rest of a sentence can help you find the right answer. Look at the words around the verb to help you work out the tense of the sentence and who or what is doing the action.

Using Rules of English — Conjunctions

Conjunctions are like glue — they join different parts of a text together.

Conjunctions Join Clauses and Sentences

1) Conjunctions join clauses together in a sentence.

> I haven't got my homework because my dog ate it.

> It was raining so Mohammed put up his umbrella.

2) Co-ordinating conjunctions are words like 'and', 'but' and 'or'.
   They join two main clauses together to make one sentence.

> You must arrive on time or the gates will be locked. ← 'or' links the two main clauses together.

3) Subordinating conjunctions are words like 'although', 'until' and 'because'.
   They join a main clause and a subordinate clause together.

> I won't set off until I'm ready.

> Although he'd reminded me, I still forgot his birthday.

Subordinating conjunctions can go at the start of sentences or between two clauses.

Since the subordinate clause in this sentence comes first, you need a comma here.

Conjunctions can be Words or Short Phrases

Conjunctions may be Short Words

These are words like 'so', 'if', 'and', 'but', 'while' and 'since'.

> Mum's going to do some baking and she would like you to help.

> Let's go for a walk today while the weather is nice.

Conjunctions may be Short Phrases

Some conjunctions are made up of more than one word.

> Wally wasn't sure where the exit was even though he had looked at the map.

> Nadine left her homework at school so that she wouldn't have to do it.

Some conjunctions Come in Pairs

Conjunctions like 'either' / 'or' and 'neither' / 'nor' are often used in pairs.

> He had to either stay with a friend or find a hotel.

> I tried neither the salmon nor the tuna.

Using Rules of English — Conjunctions

You need to **Know How to Use Conjunctions**

EXAMPLE: **Circle the most appropriate conjunction to complete each sentence.**

a) Olive's new puppy was a bundle of energy *because / but / whether / so* it certainly wasn't house-trained.

b) My bus was late again today *although / if / also / because* the driver had called in sick.

c) I'm really looking forward to the disco tonight *because / so / although / in case* I don't know what to wear.

Method — Look for the meaning of the sentence

1) Look for the <u>relationship</u> between the <u>two clauses</u> in each sentence. This gives the sentence its <u>meaning</u>.

2) Choose the best conjunction that fits the meaning of the sentence.

> a) Olive's new puppy was a bundle of energy but it certainly wasn't house-trained.

The first clause gives a positive description of Olive's new puppy...

... whilst the second clause introduces a negative point. So 'but' is the most logical conjunction to use.

> b) My bus was late again today because the driver had called in sick.

The first clause explains that the bus was late...

... and the second clause explains why. So use 'because' to introduce the explanation.

> c) I'm really looking forward to the disco tonight although I don't know what to wear.

The first clause is a positive statement...

... but the second clause makes a negative point. 'although' is the most logical conjunction to use.

Practice Questions

1) Underline the conjunctions in the passage below.

> The Amazon Rainforest covers 40% of South America, although it has decreased in size. Humans have cut down the trees because they need wood for construction and space for farms. Conservation efforts are under way to protect the rainforest and stop people from illegally cutting down the trees.

2) Circle the most appropriate conjunction to complete each sentence.

a) I often eat cereal for breakfast *as well as / as a result / either / but* I sometimes eat toast.

b) I'd like to go out to the Italian restaurant tonight, *although / therefore / because / so* Chinese is my favourite.

TEST TIP

Try out different conjunctions to see which one fits best...

If you're asked to choose the correct conjunction and aren't sure which one is correct, try putting each option in the sentence to see which one makes the most sense.

Answering Cloze Questions

Once your vocab is top-notch and you've got a sound grasp of grammar, cloze tests should be a breeze. But just in case you want a bit of extra guidance, here are some methods you can use.

Work Out what the passage is About First

EXAMPLE: **Choose the correct words to complete the passage.**

Of all the ☐ moons / ☐ stars / ☐ planets in the solar system, Mercury is the ☐ closest / ☐ close / ☐ closer

to the Sun. As a result, its surface ☐ getting / ☐ got / ☐ gets extremely hot during the day.

☐ Considering / ☐ Despite / ☐ Without these high temperatures, scientists ☐ pretend / ☐ believe / ☐ assume that ice

exists on Mercury, just as it does on Earth.

Method 1 — Look at the context of each missing word

1) Have a quick skim through the <u>whole text</u> first — this will help you work out <u>what it's about</u>, which makes it much easier to find the right answers.

2) Now look at the <u>first question</u>. Don't just look at the options — look at the <u>whole sentence</u>.

> As you read, try not to look at the options, but think for yourself what the right answers might be.

Of all the ☐ moons / ☐ stars / ☐ planets in the solar system,

← There's only one star in the solar system, so you can rule that out, but either 'moons' or 'planets' could be correct.

Mercury is the ☐ closest / ☐ close / ☐ closer to the Sun.

← But when you read the rest of the sentence, it's talking about Mercury — a planet in our solar system.

3) So the answer to the first question is '<u>planets</u>'. →

☐ moons / ☐ stars / ■ planets

■ closest / ☐ close / ☐ closer ←

4) You can use the <u>same method</u> to work out the <u>second answer</u>. The start of the sentence compares Mercury to '<u>all</u> the planets', so you know it must be the <u>most close</u>. The word for this is '<u>closest</u>', so that's your answer.

Answering Cloze Questions

Use your **Knowledge** of **Grammar**

EXAMPLE: **Method 2 — Think about rules of English**

1) For the next question you have to choose the right form of the verb 'to get'.

2) Read the whole sentence to work out whether it's in the past, present or future tense.

As a result, its surface ☐ getting / ☐ got / ☐ gets extremely hot during the day.

From the sentence alone, you can't tell what tense it should be in. You need to look for clues in the rest of the text.

3) Look for other verbs in the passage. → | exists | | is |

These are in the present tense, so our missing verb must be too.

4) 'getting' is only part of the verb — it would need 'is' in front of it to make it present tense. 'got' is past tense, so the answer is 'gets'.

☐ getting
☐ got
■ gets

It might help to answer the questions **Out of Order**

EXAMPLE: **Method 3 — Work out the meaning of the sentence**

1) Look at the next question.

☐ Considering
☐ Despite   these high temperatures, scientists...
☐ Without

This is a tricky one because you don't get many clues from this part of the sentence. Any of these options could work.

2) Before you can work out this answer, you need to work out the next answer so you understand the full sentence.

...scientists ☐ pretend / ☐ believe / ☐ assume that ice exists on Mercury...

Scientists come up with theories and back them up with evidence — they don't usually pretend or assume things.

3) You've ruled out 'pretend' and 'assume', so the answer must be 'believe'. Now that you know this, look back at the first part of the sentence.

☐ Considering
☐ Despite   these high temperatures, scientists
☐ Without

☐ pretend
■ believe that ice exists...
☐ assume

4) The sentence says that Mercury is hot, but there's ice there, so you're looking for a word that shows a contradiction. The answer is 'Despite'.

☐ Considering
■ Despite
☐ Without

Answering Cloze Questions

Check your **Spelling** carefully in cloze tests with **Missing Letters**

EXAMPLE: **Complete the text by filling in one missing letter per box.**

Although pirates are frequently portrayed as immoral and dis☐☐☐est , pirate ships

were of☐☐n run democratically. The captain and quartermaster were

el☐☐☐ed by the crew, and any plunder seized during at☐☐☐ks on other

ships was shared amongst all the sa☐☐☐rs .

Method 1 — Think about word type and meaning

1) Read through the <u>whole text</u> first and try to get an idea of what it's about.

2) Now look at the <u>first incomplete word</u> and how it fits into the sentence.

> Although pirates are frequently portrayed as immoral and dis☐☐☐est ...

The sentence is talking about how pirates are seen, so it's probably an adjective. The word 'immoral' is negative and the conjunction 'and' is used, so the missing word is probably negative too.

3) Run through some <u>negative adjectives</u> that start with '<u>dis</u>' to see if any of them <u>fit</u> with the sentence.

> dishonest

This makes sense and fits with the letters you're given. So you need to write '<u>hon</u>' in the boxes.

4) Move on to the <u>remaining words</u> and look at how they <u>fit into their sentences</u>.

> ...pirate ships were of☐☐n run democratically.

The sentence starts with 'Although', so you know it will contradict the view that pirates were immoral. A word like 'usually' would make sense here — 'often' means the same and fits with the letters you're given, so you need to fill in '<u>te</u>'.

The missing word says what was done by the crew, so it must be a verb. Looking at the sentence before, it's probably connected to democracy, so 'elected' seems like a good choice. Write in '<u>ect</u>'.

> The captain and quartermaster were el☐☐☐ed by the crew

Method 2 — Write out the full word

1) You might spot the answer <u>quickly</u>, but it can still be <u>tricky</u> to fill in the right letters.

This word is 'attacks', but when you're working quickly it's easy to make a mistake.

> ...plunder seized during at☐☐☐ks...

> at t t a ks ✗   at a c c ks ✗   at t a c ks ✓

2) Write out the <u>full word</u> on some scrap paper <u>before</u> you fill in the missing letters — it'll make it much easier to <u>spot any mistakes</u>.

> ...shared amongst all the sa☐☐☐rs .

> salers ✗   saliors ✗
> sailers ✗   sailors ✓

> sa i l o rs

Answering Cloze Questions

1) Choose the correct words to complete the passage.

At ☐ more ☐ down ☐ up to thirty metres long, blue whales are ☐ approximately ☐ definitely ☐ usually three times

the ☐ weight ☐ length ☐ height of a double-decker bus. These ☐ massively ☐ diminutive ☐ colossal marine mammals

eat four to eight tonnes of krill, tiny sea creatures, ☐ one ☐ every ☐ all day. Blue whales have

a fringe of fine plates ☐ associated ☐ detached ☐ attached to their upper jaw. To feed, they ☐ take ☐ took ☐ taken

in a huge mouthful of water and force it out ☐ between ☐ through ☐ beyond the fringe. The krill are too

☐ tiny ☐ big ☐ clever to pass between the plates, ☐ so ☐ providing ☐ then they stay in the whale's mouth.

2) Complete the text by filling in one missing letter per box.

With a groan, the sol☐☐☐r came to. His head felt as th☐☐☐h someone had been using it as a football. With a grunt of p☐☐n , he scrambled to his feet and wa☐☐☐d for the sky to stop its alarming spinning. He bent slowly and picked up his rifle, then stumbled o☐w☐rd . His inj☐☐☐d ankle made it difficult to walk quickly, but he knew he had to reach the tr☐☐ch before the next round of shelling st☐☐t☐d . Just a few more paces and he would reach safety and s☐☐☐☐er .

Don't get bogged down if you don't know a word...

If you can't work out the missing letters in a word, fill in the rest of the words in the passage first. This will give you some time to think, and it might even give you a clue to the one you left out.

Practice Questions

Now you've worked your way through the Completing Passages section, have a go at these practice questions. They'll give you a chance to put your new skills into action.

Using Rules of English

> Underline the most appropriate word from the brackets to complete each sentence. For example:
>
> **Example:** Dawit (**went** go been gone) to town today.

1. The storm (have having **has** haven't) blown down the fence.

2. We had a good time in spite (from with for **of**) the terrible music.

3. Fiona was (**treading** trodden trod tread) water for a long time.

4. The hamster hoarded the food (if but while **so**) he could eat it later.

5. The author who (written **wrote** write writing) this book is a genius.

6. (Whether Therefore **Although** Whereas) it was hot, I took my coat.

7. He was asked to (chooses chosen choosing **choose**) his favourite flavour.

8. Mel made carrot cake (despite whenever **however** neither) Afiya came to visit.

9. Timo accidentally (woked wake **woke** woken) up his baby sister.

10. We could either record the song again (but and then **or**) leave it as it is.

11. The pilot has (flew flying **flown** fly) on hundreds of planes.

12. (Except **Besides** While Likewise) going swimming, Camila likes riding her bike.

Practice Questions

Choose a Word

> Choose the correct words to complete each passage below.

Although yoga has grown in popularity in recent years, the

13. ☐ behaviour
    ☐ discipline is
    ☐ task
    ☐ course

actually thousands of years old,

14. ☐ originating
    ☐ deriving
    ☐ generating in ancient India. The term 'yoga'
    ☐ culminating

15. ☐ names
    ☐ indicates
    ☐ refers to a set of spiritual and physical practices. Yoga is often used
    ☐ describes

as a

16. ☐ construction
    ☐ model
    ☐ structure of exercise to
    ☐ form

17. ☐ append
    ☐ resolve
    ☐ deplete flexibility and strength.
    ☐ develop

As the minutes ticked by, a sense of unease

18. ☐ overthrew
    ☐ unseated
    ☐ infiltrated the camp. Ethan had
    ☐ subverted

left to

19. ☐ discover
    ☐ scout
    ☐ gather around the jungle for food an hour ago — he ought to have
    ☐ analyse

returned by now. An ominous rustling

20. ☐ unfurling
    ☐ emitting
    ☐ emanating from the undergrowth
    ☐ resulting

21. ☐ caught
    ☐ startled
    ☐ trapped the explorers unawares. As they clung
    ☐ unnerved

22. ☐ dreadfully
    ☐ scarily
    ☐ eerily to
    ☐ apprehensively

one another, they were relieved to see Ethan emerge with a beaming smile on his face.

Practice Questions

Kangaroos, a

23. ☐ symbol
☐ signature
☐ image
☐ souvenir

of Australia, are marsupials that move around

24. ☐ intently
☐ primarily
☐ fittingly
☐ initially

by hopping. While kangaroos are

25. ☐ endorsed
☐ permitted
☐ admired
☐ preserved

by tourists,

they are often regarded as a

26. ☐ pest
☐ dispute
☐ difficulty
☐ rarity

in their native Australia. This is partly due

to their

27. ☐ modest
☐ booming
☐ extortionate
☐ limited

population — in Australia, kangaroos outnumber people.

Ushuaia, in Argentina, is often

28. ☐ rewarded
☐ claimed
☐ heralded
☐ elected

as the world's southernmost city —

29. ☐ readily
☐ skilfully
☐ efficiently
☐ accordingly

, one train to Ushuaia has been named 'The End of the

World Train'. However, it could be argued that Ushuaia is

30. ☐ ungrateful
☐ unavailable
☐ undeserving
☐ unsuitable

of this accolade. The Chilean settlement of Puerto Williams, which is

31. ☐ revoked
☐ converted
☐ classed
☐ populated

as a city in Chile, is

32. ☐ marginally
☐ practically
☐ halfway
☐ fully

further south than Ushuaia.

Practice Questions

The buildings towered above Lizzie, giving her an

33. ☐ undermining
☐ infrequent feeling of
☐ acute
☐ faltering

claustrophobia. She tended to avoid large cities,

34. ☐ forsaking
☐ favouring the slower-paced
☐ gifting
☐ inclining

life and the

35. ☐ sweeping
☐ enlarging landscapes of her old home. However, as she
☐ washing
☐ developing

36. ☐ traversed
☐ straggled on, she felt herself
☐ toured
☐ strode

37. ☐ approaching
☐ furthering in confidence. Maybe
☐ succeeding
☐ gaining

moving to the city wouldn't be as scary as she had imagined.

Although it is

38. ☐ notorious
☐ considered for causing bad breath, garlic is believed to have
☐ prominent
☐ abundant

many health benefits. Some people claim it can prevent you catching a cold, though

there is

39. ☐ adequate
☐ insufficient evidence for this. According to
☐ confined
☐ sporadic

40. ☐ superstition
☐ notion
☐ faith ,
☐ fallacy

this food can

41. ☐ salvage
☐ ward off vampires, an idea which was
☐ defend
☐ guard

42. ☐ desired
☐ notified
☐ exploded
☐ popularised

by a famous novel called *Dracula*.

Practice Questions

43.
- [ ] glossed
- [ ] blinked
- [ ] glazed
- [ ] darkened

Thandiwe's eyes _____ over as she listened to Tim prattle on about how remarkable the concert had been.

44.
- [ ] Accurately
- [ ] Truthfully
- [ ] Correctly
- [ ] Righteously

, she was envious. Her attempt

45.
- [ ] avoided
- [ ] impeded
- [ ] rejected
- [ ] objected

to get a ticket had been _____ by a large crowd outside the venue. Just as

46.
- [ ] judging
- [ ] fabricating
- [ ] analysing
- [ ] defining

Thandiwe was _____ an excuse to leave, Tim

47.
- [ ] seeked
- [ ] sifted
- [ ] rummaged
- [ ] sorted

around

in his bag and produced a brand new band T-shirt, offering it to her with a smile.

48.
- [ ] Perceptive
- [ ] Ingenious
- [ ] Budding
- [ ] Reclusive

mountaineers might be surprised to learn that, while Everest is

the world's highest mountain, it is not considered to be the most difficult to climb.

49.
- [ ] acknowledged
- [ ] informed
- [ ] visualised
- [ ] admitted

Several smaller mountains, such as K2, are _____ to be more

50.
- [ ] daredevil
- [ ] treacherous
- [ ] precarious
- [ ] reckless

. This didn't stop one brave soul successfully

51.
- [ ] descending
- [ ] reducing
- [ ] declining
- [ ] plummeting

52.
- [ ] misbelief
- [ ] flummoxing
- [ ] intervention
- [ ] astonishment

K2 on skis in 2018 though, much to the _____ of his peers.

Practice Questions

Fill in Missing Letters

Fill in the missing letters to complete the words in the following passages.

53. Salt flats are vast [ ][x][p][ ][n][ ][ ][s] of salt and minerals left behind

54. when lakes dry up. Perhaps the most [ ][r][ ][a][t][ ][t][ ][k][i][n][ ]

    example is Salar de Uyuni in South America. In the right conditions, the ground

55. behaves like a mirror and [r][ ][ ][ ][l][ ][c][ ][s] its surroundings. Many

56. people [v][ ][n][ ][u][r][ ] out to experience the wonder of seeing clouds

57. [ ][n][d][ ][r][n][ ][a][t][ ] their feet or stars everywhere they turn.

---

58. After what felt like an [e][t][ ][ ][n][ ][t][ ] in the car, Tara arrived at the

    beach. She grabbed her snorkel and ran towards the ocean. As soon as she was

59. [ ][m][m][ ][r][ ][e][d] in the water, she opened her eyes and found herself

60. in a [v][ ][b][ ][ ][n][t] world of multicoloured coral and tiny fish, whose

61. scales [s][ ][i][ ][m][ ][r][ ][d] in the sunlight streaming through the water.

62. This was Tara's favourite place, and she had all summer to [m][ ][ ][v][ ][l] at it.

---

63. Robert F. Scott was an explorer who led [ ][x][ ][e][d][ ][t][ ][ ][n][s]

64. to learn more about Antarctica. [ ][o][g][ ][t][ ][e][ ] with his team,

65. he undertook the [ ][ ][a][l][ ][e][n][ ][e] of becoming the first man

66. to reach the South Pole. On the way, Scott had to [c][o][ ][t][ ][n][ ]

    with fierce weather and the knowledge that there was another explorer named

67. Roald Amundsen [s][ ][r][ ][v][ ][n][g] to get there first.

Practice Questions

68. Milo [ ][o][w][ ][r][e][ ] himself into his seat and fastened his seat belt. It was his first time on a plane, and he wasn't sure what to expect. When the

69. plane's speed rapidly [ ][n][c][ ][ ][a][s][ ][d], he instinctively closed his

70. eyes, but soon his [ ][u][r][ ][o][ ][ ][t][y] got the better of him and he slowly opened them again. He looked outside to see the cars below

71. [s][ ][r][ ][n][ ][n][g] to the size of ants. From up here, he felt like he

72. could see the [ ][n][ ][ ][r][e] world.

---

73. While common flowers like roses are held in a high [r][ ][g][ ][ ][d], there

74. are other species that are just as worthy of [a][ ][m][ ][r][a][ ][i][ ][n]. For instance, the monkey orchid has a pattern on its petals that is almost

75. [i][ ][e][n][ ][i][ ][a][l] to the face of primate. Proteas are equally intriguing.

76. Some types of protea have flowers that resemble an [e][ ][p][l][ ][d][ ][n][ ]

77. firework, and others can even [t][ ][ ][i][v][ ] in environments destroyed by fire.

---

78. Arden had always been [a][v][ ][r][ ][ ] to confrontation. She rarely had an

79. [a][ ][g][ ][ ][e][ ][t] with anyone, and never lost her temper. However, when she found out that her brother had eaten her last biscuit, she decided that

80. enough was enough. After plotting for hours, she had [d][ ][v][ ][s][ ][d]

81. a [f][ ][o][ ][p][ ][ ][ ][f] plan to get revenge — and the best part was,

82. her brother definitely wouldn't be [a][ ][t][ ][c][i][ ][a][t][ ][n][ ] it.

Practice Questions

83. Ice cream, one of life's [l__x u__e_], has been enjoyed by people

84. around the world for centuries. Although the [o___g__n] of ice cream is

85. unknown, [h i__o r___n s] have found evidence that early forms

86. were made around the globe. In Italy, it was made by [g__h e__i n_]

    various fruits and adding them to snow. In China, an ice-cream-like dish was

87. made by [c__b__n__n g] buffalo milk with other ingredients.

_____

88. The sound of the rocket's engine [w__i__r i__g] brought Yuna back

89. to her senses. She had been staring into the endless [__b__s s] for too long,

    and now the lights of the control room made her eyes ache. Blinking hard, she

90. [r e___m__d] plotting her route to the next galaxy. Suddenly, her computer

91. lit up. It had [i__t__c e__t__d] an enemy transmission — her

92. [p__r s__e__s] had picked up her trail, and they were quickly closing in.

_____

93. Of the many animals [__u r__i n_] in the depths of the ocean, the

94. giant squid is particularly elusive. Scientists have [__t__e m__t__d]

    to study these creatures for years, but they have only been able to collect a

95. [__i m__t__] amount of data. This is somewhat surprising, given the

96. squid's huge size, but less so when you [c___s i__e r] that to reach

97. its habitat, highly [___v a__c__d] underwater technology is needed.

Section Four — Comprehension

Reading the Text

Comprehension texts come in all shapes and sizes — here's how to tackle them...

Texts can be Divided into Fiction and Non-fiction

1) Fiction texts are made up by the author, and are about imaginary events and people.
2) Non-fiction texts are based on facts, and are about real people and events.
3) Here are some examples of the types of texts you might get in your reading comprehension:

Fiction Texts

Novels or Short Stories	→ You could get a short story or an extract from a novel. These texts usually have a plot, characters and a narrator.
Myths or Legends	→ These are traditional cultural stories that often involve supernatural beings or events.
Poems	→ A poem is written in lines, not prose. Most poems have a rhythm and some may rhyme.
Film or Play Scripts	→ These are mostly made up of dialogue, with some stage directions. The speaking characters' names are listed on the left side.

Prose is the opposite of poetry — it's a continuous piece of writing.

Non-fiction Texts

Autobiographies or Biographies	→ These are factual accounts of a real person's life, either written by that person (autobiography) or by someone else (biography).
Reference Books	→ An extract from an encyclopedia or history book will give the reader an explanation or information about a specific topic.
Instructions	→ Instructions are often written as a list, e.g. a recipe.
Letters	→ Letters are written correspondence from one person to another.

Reading the Text

Comprehension Questions ask you to Pick Out Details

EXAMPLE: **Method — Highlight key words**

Make sure that your highlighting doesn't slow down your reading too much.

1) As you read, scan the text looking for information which gives you the main points of the text, and highlight a few key words.

2) Key words are things that tell you who, what, where, when, why and how.

This tells you what the passage is about.

These purposes would be helpful in a 'why' question.

> Not much is known about the origins of Stonehenge. Nobody knows when it was erected, but most historians think that it must have happened between 3000 and 2000 BC. Equally, it is unclear why it was built; some scholars argue that it served a religious purpose, but others think that it was a kind of observatory, to study the movements of the stars and planets.

These dates would be helpful in a 'when' question.

3) Read the questions, using the key words that you've highlighted as signposts to help you find where the important information is in the text.

This question asks 'what reasons', so you need to look for purposes.

1) When does the text suggest Stonehenge was built?

2) What reasons does the text give for its construction?

This question asks 'when', so you need to look for dates.

Practice Questions

1) Read the passage below and then answer the questions that follow.

> 1 Joaquin couldn't believe his eyes. Standing in front of him was Eric Debuski, lead vocalist of the 'Island Sandmen'. Eric, otherwise known as Lavahead, wasn't wearing his trademark deerhunter and aviators, but there was no doubt it was him. He'd never met anyone famous before, and now he was meeting the frontman of his favourite band. It
> 5 was astounding. "Hey kid," Eric said commandingly, "you might want to try shutting that mouth." Joaquin swallowed loudly. "S-S-Sorry", he stammered, as he scanned through Eric's basket. Eric just stood back and gazed lazily, almost as if he were a normal person.

a) What is Eric Debuski's stage name?

b) What kind of place does Joaquin work in?

c) What evidence is there in the passage to suggest how Joaquin was feeling?

Sometimes you have to work things out from the text...

A text might not always state everything clearly. You might have to figure out what's happening, why something happened, where someone is or what they're feeling using clues from the passage.

Understanding the Questions

Here are some lovely pages about 'Understanding the Questions' — just my cup of tea.

Make sure you Know the Different Question Types

1) You need to use different skills for different question types.
2) Practise recognising question types so you know how to answer them.

> The same question types come up in both standard answer and multiple choice tests. See p.78-79 for more about the two question styles.

Fact Finding Questions

Fact finding questions usually use words like who, where, what, when, why and how:

> What are the names of the two brothers?
> When did the ship set sail?

You should be able to find answers to these questions simply by reading through the passage carefully.

> See p.66-67 for more advice on tricky find the facts questions

EXAMPLE: **Method — Find the facts**

1) First, you need to look at the question to find out what you are looking for. You may need to read between the lines if the answer is not obvious.

> Who is George's oldest son?

'Who' tells you that you're looking for a name. 'oldest' tells you to look for information about ages.

2) Scan the text for the information that will help you work out the answer.

Buster is the youngest, so it can't be him.

> George had four sons: Mike, Oscar, Toby and Buster. As the youngest, Buster was spoiled growing up, whilst Mike and Toby competed over who was the favourite middle child.

The oldest must be one of these four.

Mike and Toby are the middle children, so it can't be them.

3) This information shows that Oscar must be the oldest son.

Questions about Word Meanings

You might need to use your knowledge of word meanings to answer a question:

EXAMPLE: **How did Nina feel about the state of the kitchen?**

The key words in the question are 'How', 'Nina', 'feel' and 'kitchen'. They tell you what the question is asking.

Method — Think about word meanings

1) Once you know what the question is asking, you can find the information in the text:

> Tanisha was repulsed by what she saw in the kitchen.

The text tells you how she feels.

2) If the question gives you options, choose the one that has the closest meaning:

A She was delighted.
B She was appalled.
C She was disgusted.
D She was confused.

Out of all the options 'disgusted' is the closest to 'repulsed', so C is the answer.

> See p.74-75 for more advice on questions about word meaning.

Understanding the Questions

Multiple-Statement Questions

You may be given a list of statements and asked which ones are right or wrong.

EXAMPLE: **According to the text who were the last two Conservative prime ministers?**

1. Margaret Thatcher   2. Tony Blair   3. David Cameron   4. John Major

A   1 and 2
B   2 and 3
C   2 and 4 ← You need to pick out the letter which matches the correct combination of options.
D   3 and 4

Some multiple statement questions just ask for one answer, e.g. 'Which of these statements is true?'

Method — Narrow down the options

You need to work out which two options are correct, using information from the text.

> The Conservative Party dominated British politics during the 1980s and early 1990s. Margaret Thatcher was Prime Minister from 1979 to 1990, followed by John Major from 1990 to 1997. After that, the Labour Party regained power with the election of Tony Blair. They remained in power led by Gordon Brown until 2010 when the Conservatives won the vote and David Cameron came to office.

Here's one of the answers...

...and here's the other answer. So you need the letter which matches option 3 and 4 — letter D.

You'll need to use logic to answer some multiple-statement questions — see pages 71-73.

Reasoning Questions

Reasoning questions ask about the text's purpose or meaning.

You might need to use common sense to work out the answers to some reasoning questions.

1) These questions could use phrases like 'most likely' or ask you about the opinions of the author or characters.

These questions are asking about the passage's purpose.
> What is the writer's view of wine in general?
> Where would you be most likely to read this passage?

2) Questions that ask 'why' or 'what do you think' might test your own opinion. Think about the impression you get from the text's language and tone.

If a question asks you about something that isn't in the text, look for clues in the information you've been given.
> Why does Amir keep his prize a secret?
> How do you think Faziah felt when she was caught?

For questions like this, think about how you would feel in the character's place.

TEST TIP

Don't rush when you're reading the questions...

Take a moment to make sure you understand exactly what a question is asking before you answer. If you rush, you could misunderstand the question and answer it incorrectly.

Finding Hidden Facts

Some comprehension questions test your detective skills — you'll need to read very carefully.

Sometimes you'll have to **Count Up Facts**

EXAMPLE: **Read the passage and then answer the questions that follow.**

> 1   Five children — Harry, Farooq, Dimitri, Emma and Sophie — are talking about their pets and families. Harry has two sisters and a brother. The girls are both only-children, but Sophie has her pet cat, Tiger, to keep her company. Dimitri and Harry each have a dog, and everyone except Sophie has a pet fish. Farooq says he would like a cat, but
> 5   his brother is allergic to them. Dimitri has two sisters and a hamster.

    1) How many of the children have a brother? _____

    2) Who has the most pets? _____

Method — Make a table when it helps

1) Read the first question carefully. You can ignore the second question for now.

2) Read all the information you're given, picking out the facts you need to answer the first question — which children have a brother.

> Harry has two sisters and a brother.
> Farooq says he would like a cat, but his brother is allergic to them.

    Harry and Farooq each have a brother, so the answer is two.

3) Now move on to the second question. A tally chart will help you here.

4) Write down everyone's initial, then put marks next to each initial for the pets that person has.

5) Watch out for confusing information — Farooq would like a cat, but he doesn't have one.

Initials of people →

H	II
F	I
D	III
E	I
S	I

6) Read off the table to answer the question. You're looking for the person who has the most marks next to their initial.

7) The answer is Dimitri.

Some phrases can catch you out

You need to look out for phrases like these:

'All the children...'	'All the boys...'	'All the girls...'	'...apart from...'

'Kieran did not...'	'Everyone except...'	'The only one who...'

Finding Hidden Facts

You might have to work out **How Long** something took

EXAMPLE: Read the passage and then answer the question that follows.

> 1   Max and Jade had always dreamt of having a tree house at the bottom of their garden. One Friday, after school, they decided to start building one themselves. Their father agreed to help them with the work. He was a carpenter, and every day he helped his children to build a strong, safe tree house.
>
> 5   Max and Jade worked tirelessly all weekend, and by Monday they had a basic frame. After three more days of hard work, their tree house was finally complete. All that was left to do was to celebrate their achievement. They prepared a feast of sandwiches, crisps and cakes, and invited their dad as the guest of honour.

How many days did it take Max and Jade to build the tree house? _____

Method — Pick out the important bits of information

1) Read all the information you're given, and pick out the bits that are about time.

> One Friday, after school, they decided to start building... ← They started on a Friday.

> ...every day he helped...
> This one's about time, but it doesn't really tell us anything.

> ...and by Monday...
> They were still digging on Monday.

> After three more days of hard work, their tree house was finally complete.
> They finished on Thursday — three days after Monday.

2) So they started on Friday and finished on Thursday — that's seven days.

Practice Questions

Read the passage, then answer the questions that follow.

> Glen, Ali, Kim, Marta and Luca are looking out of the windows of the school bus. Glen and Marta see a pedestrian and a cat. Kim, Ali and Luca see a yellow car. Marta and Ali see a tractor. Everyone except Kim sees a cyclist.

1) Who sees the most things? _____

2) How many children see a motorised vehicle? _____

Slow and steady wins the race...

REVISION TIP These types of questions are often full of tricky wording to make sure you're reading the passage carefully. Read the text more than once to make sure you understand it all.

Understanding the Language in the Text

Imagery is just a fancy word for writing that creates a picture in your mind.

Figurative Language gives you a Picture

1) Literal language means exactly what it says.

> Dave is a real clown.

If you are talking about someone called Dave who works as a clown, then this is a literal statement.

2) Figurative language doesn't mean exactly what it says.

> Dave is a real clown.

If you're describing someone who jokes around a lot but who isn't actually a clown, then this is a figurative statement.

3) Imagery is a type of figurative language — it's language that is used to give the reader a vivid picture of something.

> The field of tulips I saw from the window was like a red carpet stretching into the distance.

This imagery makes you imagine a red carpet, and this shows you what the field of tulips was like.

> The pie was as fragrant as a rotten egg, and its crust was concrete.

This imagery helps you to imagine how bad the pie smelt...

... and this imagery tells you how hard the crust was, but you know it isn't actually made of concrete.

There are lots of different types of Imagery

A Simile says that One Thing is Like Another

1) A simile describes something by comparing it to something else.
2) Similes always use a comparing word like 'as' or 'like'.

> His anger erupted like a volcano.

The simile helps you to imagine the force of his anger.

> Jackie's cheeks were as white as snow.

This simile emphasises how white Jackie's cheeks were.

> Life is like a rollercoaster.

Life is being compared to a rollercoaster in this simile.

Understanding the Language in the Text

A **Metaphor** says that **One Thing Is Another**

1) A metaphor describes something as actually being something else.
2) It's an example of figurative writing.

Luca's eyes were deep black oily pools.

This gives a vivid description of Luca's eyes, but they're not actually deep black oily pools.

The living room was a furnace.

The living room wasn't actually a furnace, but the metaphor shows that the room was very hot.

Personification describes a **Thing** as a **Person**

Personification makes descriptions come to life.

Personification describes something that's not human as if it is a person.

The sea races up the beach.

This sounds like the sea has the ability to run.

The sun smiled on the shoppers below.

This sounds like the sun has a human expression.

Time had been kind to Raj; there was not a wrinkle on his face.

This sounds like time was deliberately nice to Raj.

Irony is often used to **Create Humour**

Verbal Irony is where the **Opposite Meaning** is meant

1) Verbal irony is where the writer means the opposite to what they have actually written.
2) You can usually tell that the writer is being ironic from the context of the writing.

We were stranded at the airport for 48 hours with no food, which was just great.

Verbal irony is similar to sarcasm.

The writer doesn't actually mean that it was great — they actually mean the opposite. This is irony.

Situational Irony is where **Unexpected Events Occur**

Situational irony is where the opposite thing happens to what the reader expects.

While the two robbers were robbing the bank, someone stole their car.

We don't expect someone to steal from the robbers. This is an example of situational irony — it is the opposite of what we expect to happen.

Section Four — Comprehension

Understanding the Language in the Text

You might have to **Work Out** what **Figurative Language** means

EXAMPLE: **Read the passage and then answer the questions that follow.**

> I set off by the early morning coach before it was yet light, and was out on the open country road when the day came creeping on, halting and whimpering and shivering, and wrapped in patches of cloud and rags of mist, like a beggar.

From 'Great Expectations' by Charles Dickens

What is meant by the phrase 'the day came creeping on'?

A The narrator was trying to move quietly.

B The narrator was being followed by a beggar.

C The early morning light was spooky.

D It got light very gradually.

Method — Rule out the wrong options

1) Read all the options carefully, and see if there are any that you can <u>rule out</u>.

> **A** The narrator was trying to move quietly. ✘ ← The phrase is about the day, not the narrator, so we can discount this one.

2) The other options seem plausible, so think about how the phrase fits into the passage.

> the day came creeping on, halting and whimpering and shivering → These words make the day seem weak and pitiful. It doesn't seem spooky, so we can discount C. → **C** The early morning light was spooky. ✘

> patches of cloud and rags of mist, like a beggar. → The author is comparing the morning to a beggar — it's a simile, so we can discount B. → **B** The narrator was being followed by a beggar. ✘

3) This leaves us with D. → **D** It got light very gradually. ✔ ← We know that it's early morning, so the day 'creeping on' means a slow dawn.

Practice Question

1) Before my eyes, the sky caught fire as the burning orb plunged into the ocean.
   What is meant by the phrase 'the sky caught fire'?

   A It was very hot.   **C** There was an explosion.

   B It was sunset.   **D** The sky was too bright to look at.

REVISION TIP

Poetry uses a lot a figurative language...

If you want to work on identifying and understanding imagery, try reading some poetry. Think about how poets manage to create pictures in your mind using language.

Multiple Statement Questions — Logic

Sometimes you need to use a bit of logic and deduction to find the answers.

Logic Questions use lots of different skills

To do well in logic questions you need to be able to:
1) Read and understand information and pay attention to details.
2) Pick out key pieces of information to solve a problem, and ignore the bits that are irrelevant.
3) Do simple maths quickly.

You can **Practise Logical Thinking** in different ways

1) Buy a puzzle magazine — these often have logic puzzles in them.
   There are puzzles like this on the internet too.
2) Play games like 'Cluedo' or 'Guess Who?' to test your powers of deduction and logic.
3) Play 'Twenty Questions' with a friend — it'll help you practise dealing with information.
4) Practise doing calculations which use addition and subtraction.

11+ Example Question

You might be asked questions like this one in the test:

EXAMPLE: **Read the passage, then answer the question that follows.**

> Aileen, Pascal, Jen, Marie and Louis are talking about their cousins.
> Marie has 3 cousins. Jen has more cousins than Louis. Aileen has one
> fewer cousin than Marie. Louis has twice the number of cousins Aileen has.
> Pascal has no aunts or uncles.

Which one of the sentences below cannot be true?

A Jen has 5 cousins.
B Pascal has the fewest cousins.
C Louis has 6 cousins.
D Aileen is Jen's cousin.

- Only one option is definitely not true.
  You need to use the information to work out which one.
- The answer is C:
  1) You're told that Marie has three cousins.
  2) Ailleen has one fewer than Marie — so she must have two cousins.
  3) Louis has twice the number of cousins Aileen has. Aileen
     has two cousins, so Louis must have four cousins, not six.

Multiple Statement Questions — Logic

Rule out the Options that are definitely Wrong

EXAMPLE: **Read the passage, then answer the question that follows.**

> "Right!" exclaimed Donald. "What are the scores, Ravi Dawes?"
> Ravi rolled his eyes and looked down at his bit of paper listing the scores.
> "Looks like I've won. Donald, you got 96, but Sascha beat you by 8 points. Ola, you scored 30 less than Sascha, and Sarah, you got 78." He screwed up the bit of paper and threw it over his shoulder. "Better luck next time, boys and girls."

Which one of the sentences below must be true?

A   Ravi scored 110.
B   Ola came last.
C   Sascha scored less than Sarah.
D   Ola had never played before.

Method 1 — Look for definite facts first

1) Look at the four options. The correct answer will be directly related to the information in the question — scan the options to see if any are unrelated.

~~D   Ola had never played before.~~ ← The passage doesn't say who has played before, so you can ignore this one.

2) To decide between the other options you'll have to do some maths to work out what each person scored. First write down any exact scores that are given in the text.

| Donald scored 96. | Sarah scored 78. |

3) Look at the rest of the passage and use the information to work out each person's score.

Sascha scored 8 more than Donald. → Donald scored 96, so Sascha scored 96 + 8 = 104.

Ola scored 30 less than Sascha. → Sascha scored 104, so Ola scored 104 − 30 = 74.

Ravi won. → This means Ravi scored more than everyone else, so he must have scored more than 104.

4) Now you know everyone's scores, write them as a list and then use the information to decide which statement is true.

Ignore any options that could be true — you're looking for the one that must be true.

Write as much of each person's name as you need to — it'll stop you getting mixed up.

R — 104+
Sas — 104
D — 96
Sar — 78
O — 74

A   Ravi scored 110. **?**
B   Ola came last. **✓**
C   Sascha scored less than Sarah. **✗**
~~D   Ola had never played before.~~

5) The only statement that must be true is B.

Multiple Statement Questions — Logic

Think about how the **Statements Fit Together**

EXAMPLE: **Read the passage and then answer the question that follows.**

> Polly was meeting Stuart, Luke, Mandy and Caitlyn at the cinema.
> Luke arrived before Caitlyn and Mandy. Polly arrived second.
> She'd hoped to get all the girls together to discuss their holiday
> plans, but the next person to turn up was a boy.

Which one of the sentences below cannot be true?

A   Stuart arrived first.   C   Mandy arrived before Polly.
B   Polly arrived before Luke.   D   Caitlyn and Mandy arrived together.

Method 2 — Look at the statements one by one

1) Read the passage. You need to work out the order in which everyone arrived.

2) You know Polly arrived second. Use the other statements
   to work out when the others arrived.

   | the next person to turn up was a boy. | → Only Luke or Stuart can arrive third.

   Luke must arrive first or third, so Caitlyn
   and Mandy must arrive fourth and fifth.

   | Luke arrived before Caitlyn and Mandy. | → If the two girls arrive fourth and fifth,
   Stuart can only arrive first or third.

3) Scribble down the order they could arrive. →

   1st — L / S
   2nd — P
   3rd — L / S
   4th — C / M
   5th — C / M

4) Use your list to choose the correct answer.
   Here you're looking for the only one that cannot be true.

5) You know Mandy must arrive after Polly, so the answer is C.

Practice Question

Read the passage and then answer the question that follows.

> Ellie, Mike, Nathan, Zach and Li are competing in a sack race on sports day.
> Mike comes fourth. Zach isn't last. Ellie doesn't win. Li beats Zach. Nathan beats Li.

1) Which one of the sentences below cannot be true?
   A   Ellie comes last.   B   Zach beats Mike.   C   Ellie falls over.   D   Li comes third.

When you know, you know...

You can narrow down the possible answers in Multiple Statement questions by discounting any
options that may or may not be true. If the text doesn't confirm it either way, it can't be the answer.

Word Meanings

Knowing lots of words will help you in the test. These pages show you how you can put your vocabulary into action when you're answering word meaning comprehension questions.

You might be asked what a word **Means**

1) If you come across a word you <u>don't know</u> in the test, don't panic — you can still get the question right. There are some <u>tricks</u> you can use to <u>work out</u> what the word means.

2) Here's an <u>example</u> of the sort of question you might be asked in the test:

EXAMPLE: **Read the passage and then answer the questions that follow.**

> The owl sat upon the bridge feeling disgruntled, staring down at her reflection in the water below. Only that morning she had been the wisest owl in the forest, but that accolade had been taken by her ecstatic sister. Her eyes suddenly focused on the pool below as a small face broke the surface.

1) What does the word 'disgruntled' mean?

A Surprised

B Annoyed

C Bored

D Confused

For these questions, you may be asked to identify the meaning of a word or phrase that appears in the text.

Use the **Passage** to help you **Work Out** the answer...

EXAMPLE: **Method 1 — Look at the rest of the passage for clues**

1) Look at the <u>context</u> of the word for clues about what it means.

> The owl sat upon the bridge feeling disgruntled, staring down at her reflection in the water below. Only that morning she had been the wisest owl in the forest, but that accolade had been taken...

The owl used to be the wisest, but she isn't any more. This is likely to make her feel upset or offended.

2) Look through the <u>options</u> for a word that means 'upset' or 'offended'.

A Surprised ✗
B Annoyed ✓
C Bored ✗
D Confused ✗

'annoyed' is the only option that has a similar meaning to 'upset', so that's the answer.

Word Meanings

EXAMPLE:

2) What does the word 'accolade' mean?
- **A** Punishment
- **B** Joyful
- **C** Trophy
- **D** Honour

Method 2 — Use word type to narrow down the options

1) Look at the context of the word and work out what type of word it is.

> It's something that has been taken, so it must be a noun. The thing that has been taken is the position of wisest owl — this isn't a physical thing that you can see or touch, so it must be an abstract noun.

> ...she had been the wisest owl in the forest, but that accolade had been taken by her ecstatic sister...

2) Narrow down the options by ruling out words that aren't abstract nouns.

- **A** Punishment
- **B** Joyful ✗
- **C** Trophy ✗
- **D** Honour

> 'Joyful' is an adjective, and 'trophy' is a common noun. 'Punishment' and 'honour' can both be abstract nouns, so you need to think about what they mean.

3) The text tells you that the 'accolade' is the position of wisest owl. This is a good thing, so 'punishment' doesn't make sense. The answer must be 'honour'.

Practice Questions

Read the passage below and then answer the questions that follow.

> Laura glanced down at the ground far below her and gulped. Mrs Parry had pleaded so fervently for her help that she hadn't felt able to refuse. But now, with the ladder wobbling alarmingly, she was starting to regret her benevolence. Next time, she thought grimly, she'd be more circumspect about offering to rescue cats from trees.

1) What does the word 'fervently' mean?

A Emotionally　　**B** Calmly　　**C** Angrily　　**D** Joyfully

2) What does the word 'circumspect' mean?

A Forethought　　**B** Anxiety　　**C** Enthusiastic　　**D** Cautious

---

REVISION TIP

These methods can help you to work out the answer...

...but sometimes you just have to know what a word means. Building up your vocabulary will make it easier to answer these word meaning comprehension questions in the test.

Reasoning Questions

Reasoning questions ask you to look beyond the facts you're given in the text.

You might be asked about the **Writer's Purpose**

EXAMPLE: **Read the passage and then answer the questions that follow.**

> **Brushes with Nature** by Hilary Powell, Tibworth Tourist Board
>
> Award-winning wildlife painter Jack Jones opens an inspirational new exhibition in Tibworth today, charting a year in the life of a family of foxes who live at the bottom of his garden. Jack's last exhibition, 'Frogspawn', was described as 'a stunning portrayal of the transient nature of life'.

1) Why do you think the writer chose the title 'Brushes with Nature'?

A Jack Jones wants to clean up nature reserves. 　　C The article is about painting.

B It sums up both of the article's topics. 　　D Foxes' tails are called brushes.

Method 1 — Rule out the wrong options

1) Read through all the options carefully and rule out any wrong ones.

> **A** Jack Jones wants to clean up nature reserves. ✘ ←── The article doesn't say anything about nature reserves, so you can rule out A.

Both painting and foxes are mentioned in the article, but they're not the only reason the author chose the title, so C and D aren't right. ──→
> **C** The article is about painting. ✘
> **D** Foxes' tails are called brushes. ✘

2) That just leaves B.

> **B** It sums up both of the article's topics. ✔ ←── The article is about wildlife painting, so art and nature are its topics. The title sums these up, so this is the answer.

EXAMPLE: **2) Why do you think the writer uses the words 'inspirational' and 'Award-winning'?**

A She is a big fan of Jack Jones. 　　C She wants people to visit the exhibition.

B Jack Jones inspired her to paint. 　　D She really enjoyed the exhibition.

Method 2 — Look at all the evidence

1) All these options could be true, but the article doesn't say that any of them are.

2) Sometimes, there's a bit of information hidden away that gives you a clue to the answer.

> by Hilary Powell, Tibworth Tourist Board ←── This gives you a big clue about why Hilary wrote the article. She works for the tourist board, so her job is to encourage people to visit Tibworth.

The exhibition could bring more people to Tibworth, so the answer is C. ──→
> **C** She wants people to visit the exhibition. ✔

Reasoning Questions

You might have to **Work Out** how a **Character Feels**

EXAMPLE: **Read the passage and then answer the questions that follow.**

> Kazim crouched behind the sofa as the footsteps approached, hardly daring to breathe. He closed his eyes and pictured the room, trying to remember whether he had left any trace of his presence. The footsteps stopped right in front of his hiding place, and Kazim jumped as a voice began to speak.

Which of these words best describes how Kazim feels?

A Disappointed   **B** Unhappy   **C** Tense   **D** Sneaky

Method — Put yourself in the character's place

1) Read the passage carefully. As you read, <u>imagine</u> you are doing what the character does. Think about <u>why</u> he's doing it, and how he might <u>feel</u>.

Kazim is hiding — he doesn't want to be seen.

> Kazim crouched behind the sofa as the footsteps approached, hardly daring to breathe.

The words 'hardly daring' show that it's a serious situation. Kazim really doesn't want to be found.

These actions don't really describe someone who is disappointed, so you can rule out A.

You'd only jump at the sound of a voice if you were on edge.

> Kazim jumped as a voice began to speak

2) Look through all the <u>options</u> and pick the one that seems <u>most accurate</u>. Kazim is <u>hiding</u>, and he's <u>on edge</u>. The best adjective is '<u>tense</u>', so the answer is <u>C</u>.

Practice Question

Read the passage and then answer the questions that follow.

> The wind roared furiously around the cliffs, whipping the white-capped waves to a hissing, boiling frenzy. Leaning forward into the gale, Isla scanned the horizon feverishly. Where were they? They should have reached the far side of the lake by now. In the distance, a tiny speck of light appeared, flashed twice, and then disappeared. Isla let out a breath she didn't know she'd been holding.

1) Which of these words best describes the mood the writer creates in the passage?

A Frightening   **B** Anxious   **C** Miserable   **D** Bitter

Actions speak louder than words...

REVISION TIP

Writers often try to show a character's emotions through their actions. Reading lots of fiction will help you become more familiar with working out what characters are feeling.

Answering Comprehension Questions

There are two different types of question — multiple choice or standard answer.

Multiple Choice Questions give you Several Possible Options

1) In multiple choice questions you'll get options to choose from. You need to pick the right answer.
2) When the possible options are similar, it can make the question more difficult.
   The best way to tackle each question is to work through it carefully, step by step.

EXAMPLE: **Read the passage below. Then answer the question that follows.**

1   The problem was not that the film was three hours long, or that the acting was
    atrocious, but that the plot was incomprehensible. I have no idea what Captain Jutter
    had to do with anything, partly because I could not understand a word he said, but
    also because he disappeared halfway through the film, without any explanation. I
5   don't think it was ever explained why the pirates had to get back to Shadow Island;
    all I know is that it was of "great importance". The screenwriter, Jordan Vidal, needs
    to take a long, hard look in the mirror after this terrible mishap of an adventure film.

1) According to the passage, what was the film's biggest flaw?

   A The screenwriter was not very good.
   B The acting was terrible.
   C It didn't make any sense.
   D It was too long.

> Be wary of options that are mentioned in the text but don't answer the question, as they could mislead you. Always double-check that your answer matches the text.

Method 1 — Find the important information

1) First, look for any key words relating to the question
   (you may have highlighted them during your first read-through):

'problem' means a similar thing to 'flaw'.

> The problem was not that the film was three hours long, or that the acting was atrocious, but that the plot was incomprehensible.

This sentence mentions three possible answers to the question.

The sentence tells you that the problem was not the length of the film or the acting, so it cannot be option B or D.

2) Check this information against the options.

   A The screenwriter was not very good.
   B ~~The acting was terrible.~~
   C It didn't make any sense.
   D ~~It was too long.~~

Option C is closest in meaning to the text — 'incomprehensible' means 'doesn't make any sense'.

3) Double-check you haven't missed anything else. The last line of the passage does suggest that the screenwriter was not very good (option A), but C is still the best answer.

Answering Comprehension Questions

Use Your Own Words for Standard Answer Questions

1) <u>Standard answer comprehension questions</u> aren't <u>too different</u> from multiple choice questions.

2) You can find the answers in the <u>same way</u>, but instead of choosing a given answer, you need to put it into your <u>own words</u> and write in <u>full sentences</u>.

3) <u>Read</u> the <u>extract</u> on p.78, and then look at the question below.

You'll probably get multiple choice options in the test, but it's worth knowing how to answer standard answer questions too.

EXAMPLE: **2) Explain why the writer found the plot "incomprehensible" (line 2).**

Method 2 — Ask yourself questions as you're reading

1) First, work out <u>what information</u> the question is asking you for:

> Explain why the writer found the plot "incomprehensible" (line 2)?

This gives you a clue to where to start looking for the answer.

This tells you that you're looking for reasons why the writer didn't understand the story.

2) You should <u>start</u> by looking at the part of the text <u>mentioned</u> in the <u>question</u>:

> I have no idea what Captain Jutter had to do with anything, partly because I could not understand a word he said, but also because he disappeared halfway through the film, without any explanation.

This sentence comes straight after the writer mentions that the story was "incomprehensible".

Finding key words will help you work out what's important.

This sentence tells you that the writer <u>did not know why</u> Captain Jutter was in the film, because he <u>could not understand</u> what he said, and he <u>disappeared</u> halfway through.

3) After looking around line 2, you should then <u>check</u> the <u>key words</u> in the <u>rest of the text</u>:

> I don't think it was ever explained why the pirates had to get back to Shadow Island...

The word 'explained' suggests that this sentence relates to the plot.

4) After you have <u>all the information</u>, <u>rewrite</u> it in <u>full sentences</u>, in your <u>own words</u>:

> The plot was "incomprehensible" because the writer did not know why Captain Jutter was in the film, and found it impossible to understand him. The writer was also confused because Captain Jutter vanished in the middle of the film, and it was not explained why the pirates needed to go to Shadow Island.

Quoting from the question helps focus your answer.

Change the wording so you're not just copying the text.

5) Use the <u>number of marks</u> and <u>space available</u> for your answer as a guide for <u>how much</u> to write.

TEST TIP — Try to answer every question, but use your time well...

You should answer as many questions as you can, but don't spend too long on a question if you can't work out the answer — make a sensible guess and move on to the next question.

Practice Questions

There's lots to revise in the Comprehension section, so have a go at these questions to see how well you've taken things in. If you get a question wrong, reread the relevant pages then try again.

Finding Hidden Facts

> Read the information carefully, then use it to answer the question that follows. Write your answer on the line.

1. Sami, Jorge, Maya, Luke and Eve are choosing toppings for their burgers.

    Luke and Jorge have tomato on top of their burger. Maya is the only one who doesn't have onions. Everyone except Sami puts cheese on their burger. Only Maya and Jorge have bacon.

    Who has the **most** toppings on their burger? _____

2. Tori, Kim, Dennis, Ling and Uri are comparing all the places they have visited.

    Everyone has visited Manchester. Uri is the only one who hasn't been to Edinburgh. Dennis and Ling visited Cornwall together last year. Kim has also been to Cornwall, and she's the only person who has been to Bath. Tori and Kim have been to Kendal.

    Who has been to the **fewest** places? _____

3. Rashid, Charlie, Harry, Sona and Anita are discussing their hobbies.

    Only Charlie bakes. Everyone does swimming apart from Anita and Harry. Rashid, Charlie, Sona and Harry all play hockey. Anita goes to boxing classes with Sona. Only Anita plays the piano. Nobody except Sona does cycling.

    Who does the **most** hobbies? _____

4. Rob, Bianca, Violet, Chad and Georgia are discussing their favourite film genres.

    Rob and Bianca like comedy. Neither Georgia nor Chad like horror, but everyone else does. Everyone is a fan of romance films except for Rob. Georgia and Violet both like sci-fi. Bianca is the only one who enjoys action films.

    Who likes the **most** genres? _____

Practice Questions

5. Anwar, Monique, Wes, Hank and Shirley are all in a painting class together.

    Hank is the only person who is using purple paint. Monique, Wes and Anwar are all using black. Shirley is the only one who isn't using yellow paint. Everyone is using white in their paintings except for Anwar. Wes and Hank are not using any blue paint, but everyone else is.

    Who is using the **fewest** colours? _____

6. James, William, Ella, Phoebe and Sasha are helping with jobs around the house.

    James and William both cleaned the bathroom. Ella tidied the kitchen and the lounge. Everyone cleaned the dining room except Sasha. Phoebe helped to tidy the lounge. Ella and James both cleaned the garage. Sasha was the only one who tidied the hall.

    Who helped out in the **most** rooms? _____

7. Mhairi, Gwen, Anders, Emily and Shawn are bringing food to a birthday party.

    Mhairi and Gwen brought potato salad. Everyone except Gwen brought crisps and sandwiches. Anders brought sausage rolls, cookies and brownies. Emily supplied the birthday cake. Shawn brought brownies as well as pizza.

    Who brought the **most** food to the party? _____

8. Philip, Victor, Theresa, Hector and Erin have gone to the market.

    Erin, Theresa and Hector bought oranges. Everyone bought apples and peaches except for Hector who only bought peaches. Philip bought bananas, grapes and pears. Hector also bought grapes and pears, as well as some strawberries.

    Who bought the **fewest** types of fruit? _____

Section Four — Comprehension

Practice Questions

Multiple-Statement Questions

Read the information carefully, then use it to answer the question that follows. Circle the letter of the correct option for each question.

9. Luca, Helen, Tessa, Maren and Jasper are collecting shells on the beach. Luca collects the second highest number of shells. Helen collects fewer shells than Tessa. Jasper collects more shells than Luca.

    Which one of the sentences below **must** be true?

    A   Jasper collected the most shells.

    B   Maren and Jasper collected the same number of shells.

    C   Tessa didn't collect any shells.

    D   Maren collected the fewest shells.

10. Naomi, Craig, Li, Petra and Maria are talking about their pets. Petra has twice as many pets as Li. Maria has one fewer pet than Petra. Li has two pets. Craig and Naomi both have the same number of pets as Maria.

    Which one of the sentences below **cannot** be true?

    A   Petra has four pets.

    B   Maria has three dogs.

    C   Craig and Naomi are siblings.

    D   Naomi has fewer pets than Li.

11. Orla, John, Anza, Ellie and Imani are racing each other to the shops. Anza doesn't come fourth. Anza beats Orla. Ellie comes third. John reaches the shops before Anza.

    Which one of the sentences below **cannot** be true?

    A   John is the winner.

    B   Orla beats Ellie.

    C   Imani comes last.

    D   Orla runs faster than Imani.

Practice Questions

12. Pascal, Jessie, Summer, Luke and Anthony are all on the same bus. Luke got on the bus at 5.45. Anthony got on the bus twenty minutes after Luke. Jessie got on ten minutes after Anthony. Pascal was the first one of them to get on the bus. Luke got on half an hour before Summer.

    Which one of the sentences below **must** be true?

    A   The bus was running late.

    B   Anthony was the last person to get on the bus.

    C   Pascal and Luke got on the bus together.

    D   Summer and Jessie got on the bus at the same time.

13. Bella, Frankie, Ray, Denny and Gemma are sharing a plate of six apples and six pears. Bella ate an apple and a pear. Frankie ate two pears. Ray had one apple and two pears. Gemma ate three apples.

    Which one of the sentences below **cannot** be true?

    A   Gemma would have preferred a pear.

    B   Denny ate two apples and a pear.

    C   Frankie ate twice as many pears as Bella.

    D   Denny had an apple.

14. Hazim, Rachel, Thandi, Ash and Kingsley are comparing their marks from their biology test. Thandi got the highest mark. Ash scored fifteen marks fewer than Thandi. Rachel scored 75, five marks more than Ash. Hazim came last with a score of 58.

    Which one of the sentences below **must** be true?

    A   Kingsley and Hazim came joint last.

    B   Ash got 80 marks.

    C   Thandi scored 85 marks.

    D   Kingsley failed the test.

Practice Questions

Word Meanings

Read the passage below, then answer the questions that follow.
Underline the correct option for each question.

Adapted extract from 'The Errand Boy' by Horatio Alger Jr.

Phil Brent was plodding through the snow in the direction of his house when
a snowball, moist and hard, struck him just below his ear with stinging emphasis.
The pain was considerable, and Phil's anger rose.

He turned suddenly, his eyes flashing fiercely, intent upon discovering who had
5 committed this outrage. His ears gave him the first clue. He heard a chuckle, which
seemed to proceed from behind the stone wall that ran along the roadside.

"I will see who it is," he decided, and plunging through the snow he surmounted the
wall, in time to see a boy of about his own age running away across the fields as fast as
the deep snow would allow.

10 "It's you, Jonas!" he shouted wrathfully. "I thought it was a sneaking fellow like you."

The freckled face of Jonas Webb, his step-brother, showed a degree of dismay, for he
had not calculated on discovery. Jonas ran the faster, but while fear winged his steps,
anger proved the more effectual spur, and Phil overtook him.

15. In the context of the text, what does "proceed from" (line 6) mean?

   A Come from   **B** Continue from   **C** Advance from   **D** Burst from

16. What does "wrathfully" (line 10) mean?

   A Loudly   **B** Forcefully   **C** Furiously   **D** Impatiently

17. In the context of the passage, what does the word "dismay" (line 11) mean?

   A Terror   **B** Alarm   **C** Horror   **D** Defiance

18. What does the phrase "fear winged his steps" (line 12) suggest about Jonas?

   A He was afraid of being chased.   **C** His fear made him run faster.
   B His fear made him stumble.   **D** He was jumping into the air as he ran.

Practice Questions

Comprehension Questions

Read the passage below, then answer the questions that follow.

The Secret of the Lost Tomb

My name is Aurelia Martin and I was twelve years old when my mum became one of the most famous archaeologists in the world. On a sweltering Tuesday in the middle of the desert, she unearthed an ancient tomb filled with artefacts that changed the world's perception of Ancient Egypt forever.

5   It was four years ago to the day. My mum and I woke promptly to take advantage of the cool morning conditions, and drove the twenty miles out to the dig site, two hours before the rest of her team had even climbed out of their soft beds.

Not long after midday, I was watching my mum carefully excavating what looked like a slab of sandstone. Suddenly, she jumped up, grabbed me around the waist and pulled
10   me backwards. Right where she had been digging, a patch of sand started to flow into a hole in the ground, like a waterfall racing over the edge of a cliff. In a matter of seconds, the mouth of a tunnel had appeared in the middle of the sandy expanse, yawning up at the clear Egyptian sky.

After ensuring it was safe, my mum and her colleagues spent the next three hours
15   heaving tools into the passageway while I sat in the shade twiddling my thumbs. After what felt like an eternity, my mum's dirt-smudged face emerged and she called me over.

By now, the sun was blazing down on the arid expanse, and a dry wind was sporadically whipping up clouds of sand. But the second I stepped tentatively into the passageway, the air turned cool and still. I shivered and moved closer to my mum, my
20   eyes darting around the mysterious tunnel. As we walked, the sound of footsteps echoed eerily, like an army of ghosts marching up the passageway to meet us. Before long, the narrow space opened out into a vast chamber. The walls were adorned with paintings in bright hues of red, blue and yellow. Nine massive stone pillars bolstered the ceiling, each one covered in hieroglyphics that I couldn't read. But the most impressive part was
25   the row of towering carved figures, standing like sentries over a rectangular stone box. They must have been three times my height and spanned the entire back wall of the tomb.

"We're the first people to stand in this room for over four thousand years," my mum said as my mouth fell open. It felt as though we'd stepped back in time.

Practice Questions

Answer these questions about the text.
Circle the letter of the correct option for each question.

19. According to the text, how old is Aurelia now?

    A   Eight

    B   Twelve

    C   Fifteen

    D   Sixteen

20. Why did Aurelia's mum pull her backwards in lines 9-10?

    A   She wanted to get Aurelia out of danger.

    B   She was playing with Aurelia.

    C   Aurelia was in her way.

    D   Aurelia was standing on an important artefact.

21. The phrase "twiddling my thumbs" (line 15) suggests that Aurelia is:

    A   nervous because she is worried that her mum might be in danger.

    B   impatient because she wants to see the passageway.

    C   bored because she has nothing to do.

    D   excited because she knows her mum has discovered something special.

22. Which of the following statements cannot be true?

    A   Aurelia and her mum discovered the tomb on a weekday.

    B   It was two o'clock in the afternoon when Aurelia entered the tunnel.

    C   They discovered the tunnel on the second day of excavations.

    D   Aurelia and her mum left for the dig site before dawn.

23. What does the word "sporadically" (line 18) mean?

    A   Regularly

    B   Intermittently

    C   Consistently

    D   Rapidly

Practice Questions

24. Why do you think Aurelia "shivered" (line 19) when she entered the tunnel?

   A   The tunnel was freezing.

   B   She was afraid of the dark.

   C   She felt uneasy.

   D   The tunnel was haunted.

25. The statues were "standing like sentries" (line 25). This suggests they:

   A   looked as if they were praying.

   B   looked like they were guarding the stone box.

   C   appeared to be in mourning.

   D   had serious expressions on their faces.

26. Which of the following statements must be true?

   A   Aurelia had never been in an Ancient Egyptian tomb before.

   B   The floor of the tomb was covered in sand.

   C   The rectangular stone box contained a mummy.

   D   The ceiling of the tomb was too high for Aurelia to touch.

27. In line 28, the narrator says "It felt as though we'd stepped back in time." What does this suggest about the tomb?

   A   The tomb was crumbling and decaying.

   B   It was the oldest tomb they had ever been in.

   C   The tomb wasn't as old as Aurelia's mum thought.

   D   The tomb looked as it did when it was first built.

28. Which word best describes how the narrator is feeling at the end of the passage?

   A   Anxious

   B   Eager

   C   Awed

   D   Proud

Mixed Practice Tests

If you want to attempt each mixed practice test more than once, you will need to print **multiple-choice answer sheets** for these questions from our website — go to www.cgpbooks.co.uk/11plusanswersheets. If you'd prefer to answer them in standard write-in format, follow the instructions in the tests.

Give yourself **12 minutes** to complete this test. Write down your score in the box at the end.

Test 1

Read this poem carefully and answer the questions that follow.

An adapted extract from 'The Paper Kite'

Once on a time, a paper kite
Was mounted to a wondrous height;
Where, giddy with its elevation,
It thus expressed self-admiration:
5 "See how those crowds of gazing people
Admire my flight above the steeple;
How would they wonder, if they knew
All that a kite, like me, could do?
Were I but free, I'd take a flight,
10 And pierce the clouds beyond their sight.
But, ah! like a poor prisoner bound,
My string confines me near the ground.
I'd brave the eagle's towering wing,
Might I but fly without a string."
15 It tugged and pulled, while thus it spoke,
To break the string — at last it broke!

Deprived at once of all its stay*,
In vain it tried to soar away:
Unable its own weight to bear,
20 It fluttered downward through the air;
Unable its own course to guide,
The winds soon plunged it in the tide.
Oh! foolish kite, you had no wing,
How could you fly without a string?

by Marmaduke Park

*stay — *support*

Answer these questions about the poem that you've just read.
Circle the letter of the correct option for each question.

1. Which of the words below best describes how the kite feels in lines 1-4?

    A   Reckless
    B   Alert
    C   Unsteady
    D   Confident

Mixed Practice Tests

2. According to the poem, which of the following statements is true?

   A   The kite is impressed by the crowds below.
   B   The crowds want to know what else the kite can do.
   C   The kite thinks that the crowds are in awe of it.
   D   The crowds are admiring the steeple.

3. Which of the following best describes what the kite wants to do in lines 9-14?

   A   Fly freely
   B   See through the clouds
   C   Fly very quickly
   D   Hide from the crowds

4. In line 13, the kite would "brave the eagle's towering wing".
   What does this suggest about the kite?

   A   The kite thinks that eagles are more courageous than itself.
   B   It sees eagles as the enemy.
   C   It wants to confront an eagle.
   D   It would risk flying up high where the eagles are.

5. Look at lines 19-22. Which of the following statements is false?

   A   The kite couldn't control its movements.
   B   The kite can't stay in the air on its own.
   C   The kite fell smoothly to the ground.
   D   The wind cast the kite into the sea.

6. Which of the following is not mentioned in the poem?

   A   A church tower
   B   A bird
   C   The sea
   D   A jail

7. What does the word "elevation" (line 3) mean in the context of the poem?

   A   Splendour
   B   Altitude
   C   Importance
   D   Gliding

8. What does "In vain" (line 18) mean in the context of the poem?

   A   Without hope
   B   In a reckless way
   C   Without success
   D   In an arrogant way

Mixed Practice Tests

Find the word that means the opposite, or nearly the opposite, of the word on the left. Underline your answer. Look at this example:

Example: **worried**   confident <u>calm</u> assured elated

9. **perpetual**   scarce momentary sudden frequent

10. **disobey**   discharge petition comply ignore

11. **inquisitive**   timid uninterested secretive trusting

12. **passionate**   uninvolved critical apathetic reluctant

13. **mobile**   stationary locked unyielding listless

14. **quarrelsome**   mindful approachable silent cooperative

Find the word that means the same, or nearly the same, as the word on the left. Underline your answer. Look at this example:

Example: rural   urban <u>rustic</u> quiet wild

15. **abnormal**   frightening outlandish abrupt improbable

16. **bewildering**   odd distressing mystifying tiresome

17. **convenient**   opportune sublime proficient functional

18. **unnerve**   confound surprise perturb disarrange

19. **resistant**   invincible protective forceful immune

20. **disclose**   unleash suggest divulge coordinate

21. **harsh**   feared strident menacing boorish

Total (out of 21):

Mixed Practice Tests

Give yourself **12 minutes** to complete this test. Write down your score in the box at the end.

Test 2

Three of the words in each list are linked. Underline the word that is not related to these three. Look at this example:

Example: lake   ocean   <u>shore</u>   stream

1. habit   preference   practice   routine

2. fable   legend   fairytale   dictionary

3. luminous   searing   radiant   incandescent

4. nourished   guzzled   devoured   gorged

5. javelin   spear   arrow   dart

Complete the word on the right so that it means the opposite, or nearly the opposite, of the word on the left. Look at this example:

Example: hardy   f r a i l

6. **attractive**   r □ □ u g □ □ n t

7. **expedite**   □ e □ a y

8. **sceptical**   g □ l □ □ b l □

9. **counterfeit**   a □ □ h e □ t i □

10. **praise**   □ d m □ n □ s □

Mixed Practice Tests

Rearrange the words so that each sentence makes sense. Underline the word which doesn't fit into the sentence. Look at this example:

Example: the quiet very is <u>read</u> library

11. mud under the loudly rain squelched shoes my

12. across cheetahs until determinedly three sprinted savannah the

13. slowly storm be seemed the abating to after

14. her relinquish Anna book which to refused favourite

Choose the correct words to complete the passage below.

Nora stumbled through the forest, the numbness in her hands and feet

15. **A** increasing
    B reacting
    C subsiding   to
    D spreading

the rest of her body. Dark trees

16. **A** rooted
    B imparted
    C loomed   all around her, their boughs drooping under
    D branched

the

17. **A** heavy
    B heaps
    C burden   of the snow. The light was
    D drifts

18. **A** shifting
    B fading
    C brightening   quickly, and Nora
    D wavering

knew it wouldn't be long before nightfall. With each passing minute, her fear intensified —

she needed to make it back to her cabin before dark, but she was

19. **A** falteringly
    B frequently
    C undeniably
    D intentionally

lost. Earlier that day, she had taken her

20. **A** average
    B likely
    C accustom   route to search for firewood,
    D normal

Mixed Practice Tests

but she'd become distracted by the tracks of an Arctic hare and had deviated from the

21. **A** Meanwhile
    B Unfortunately
path.   **C** Presently   , a blizzard had begun soon afterwards, and the snow had
    D Lately

22. **A** obscured
    B deposited
    C enhanced   the trail that she had left behind. Now that the storm had ended, there
    D repressed

                                        23. **A** risk
                                            B hazard
was little that Nora could do to get herself out of   **C** danger   . Her only option was to
                                            D insecurity

                                24. **A** contrasting
                                    B varying
struggle onwards, the stillness of the forest   **C** whispering   with the harsh sound of her
                                    D consoling

                                        25. **A** awareness
                                            B attention
breathing. Suddenly, she froze. A noise had attracted her   **C** perception .
                                            D thoughts

                        26. **A** sense
                            B translate
Although it was faint, she could   **C** locate   it easily — it was the howling of a wolf.
                            D identify

                                    27. **A** severity
                                        B exertion
With a gasp, Nora hurried on, her muscles burning from the   **C** stretch . Just as she was
                                        D forcing

                                            28. **A** between
                                                B against
thinking she would have to shelter in a tree overnight, the forest opened up   **C** within
                                                D into

a clearing, and there was her cabin, the lantern flickering on the porch, welcoming her home.

Total (out of 28):

Mixed Practice Tests

Give yourself **12 minutes** to complete this test. Write down your score in the box at the end.

Read this passage carefully and answer the questions that follow.

The International Space Station

Have you ever wondered what it would be like to live in space? Over 250 miles above our heads, a team of astronauts are doing exactly that. They live and work aboard the International Space Station (ISS), which orbits our planet at a staggering 17 000 miles per hour — that's more than twenty times the speed of sound. The ISS orbits the Earth roughly
5 every ninety minutes, meaning those on board see the sun rise sixteen times a day.

The ISS is made up of central modules where the astronauts live and work. Attached to this central portion are several solar arrays — special panels which convert sunlight into the electricity needed to power the station. Onboard laboratories enable astronauts to carry out ground-breaking scientific research that can only be conducted in space. The astronauts
10 themselves are also test subjects, as scientists on Earth monitor how life in space affects their health. Floating around a space station all day may sound fun, but it can have a huge impact on an astronaut's body. Understanding the effects of zero-gravity (weightlessness caused by a lack of gravity) on the body enables scientists to find new ways to keep people safe in space.

Not every experiment takes place within the station; sometimes the crew set up
15 experiments outside. With no air and very little gravity, experiments can have very different outcomes in space than they would on Earth. However, space is an unforgiving place, and astronauts need to wear spacesuits to keep them safe from the dangers of open space. Unlike Earth, space has no atmosphere to keep the temperature stable, so the suits are needed to protect the astronaut from the huge fluctuations in temperature that they are exposed to. It can
20 be as hot as 120 °C in direct sunlight — that's hotter than boiling water — whereas in the shade, the temperature can plummet to –150 °C. Crucially, the spacesuits also provide the astronaut with oxygen to breathe while they are floating in the vacuum of space. Astronauts are usually tethered to the ISS, but if they were to become separated, their spacesuit is equipped with a thruster (like a mini-jetpack) that they can use to propel themselves back to the station. It's no
25 wonder that these sophisticated suits are sometimes described as one-person spaceships.

Answer these questions about the text that you've just read.
Circle the letter of the correct option for each question.

1. According to the text, the ISS travels at "more than twenty times the speed of sound" (line 4). This means that the ISS:

   A   makes a very loud sound as it travels through space.
   B   is louder than everything else in space.
   C   travels incredibly quickly.
   D   travels at the same speed as sound does.

Mixed Practice Tests

2. Which of the following statements cannot be true?

   A   There is very little gravity in space.
   B   The ISS is powered by sunlight.
   C   Zero-gravity can negatively affect an astronaut's health.
   D   The ISS circles the Earth twenty times every twenty-four hours.

3. Why are the astronauts described as "test subjects" (line 10)?

   A   They test their scientific equipment frequently.
   B   They perform experiments all the time.
   C   They carry out tests on each other.
   D   Their health is closely observed by scientists.

4. According to the text, why is it useful for astronauts to perform experiments outside?

   A   They can see if the results are different outside the ISS.
   B   They can harness the power of the sun.
   C   They can learn more about the effects of the conditions in space.
   D   They can protect their own health.

5. According to the text, which of the following is not a
   reason why the astronauts have to wear spacesuits?

   A   To allow them to breathe in space
   B   To travel between the ISS and spaceships
   C   To allow them to return to the space station in an emergency
   D   So they are shielded from the large temperature variations in space

6. Which of the following statements must be true?

   A   The spacesuits can protect against extreme heat and extreme cold.
   B   Astronauts can adjust the inner temperature of their spacesuits.
   C   The ISS has no power when there is no sunlight.
   D   Astronauts must wear spacesuits at all times.

7. What does "ground-breaking" (line 9) mean?

   A   Earth-shattering
   B   Extremely important
   C   Cutting-edge
   D   Ill-advised

8. What does the word "sophisticated" (line 25) mean?

   A   Advanced
   B   Expensive
   C   Impressive
   D   Technical

Mixed Practice Tests

Find the word that means the opposite, or nearly the opposite, of the word on the left. Underline your answer. Look at this example:

Example: **worried**   confident <u>calm</u> assured elated

9. **pristine**   defunct sullied felonious mangled

10. **adore**   abdicate condemn abhor vilify

11. **welcomed**   disallowed shunned dissuaded forgot

12. **broken**   durable malfunctioning operational unabridged

13. **favourable**   passable salvageable catastrophic disadvantageous

14. **outgoing**   introverted lethargic discreet prudent

15. **required**   invaluable trivial dispensable inaccessible

Choose the word that has a similar meaning to the words in both sets of brackets. Underline your answer. Look at this example:

Example: (wrap package) (fill load)   <u>pack</u> envelop carton crate

16. (corrupt unethical) (putrid decaying)   fetid wily crooked rotten

17. (squash squeeze) (throng crowd)   crush mob group horde

18. (sincere heartfelt) (profound weighty)   difficult truthful serious potent

19. (awkward difficult) (opposing conflicting)   intolerant contrary differing divergent

20. (cure treatment) (solve right)   remedy medicine salve result

21. (construct make) (figure shape)   produce physique build fashion

Total (out of 21):

Mixed Practice Tests

Give yourself **12 minutes** to complete this test. Write down your score in the box at the end.

Test 4

Read this passage carefully and answer the questions that follow.

The New Arrival

When Jamie found out that he was getting a little sister, he was utterly dismayed. He couldn't understand why his parents would want another child — after all, he was perfect, and therefore impossible to improve upon. What's more, he'd been here first. Why should he have to vie for his parents' attention?

5   For months, he had refused to engage in any activity that was remotely to do with the baby. When his mum had announced that she was pregnant and had offered him a piece of cake to celebrate, he'd declined it with a grimace. When his parents had invited him to help choose decorations for his sister's bedroom, he'd shrugged and wandered off, leaving his parents to make the decisions themselves.

10   Now, as Jamie sat in his grandparents' car on the way to the hospital, he could avoid meeting his sister no longer. The moment was imminent, and there was no escaping it. All he could do was cross his arms and glare out of the window.

Far too soon, he was making his way up the steps towards the main entrance. Noticing Jamie's mood, his grandma pointed across the reception area to the gift shop display.

15   "Look at those lovely flowers!" she exclaimed. "Shall we get some for your mum, Jamie?"

A grunt was all that Jamie's grandma received in response.

A few minutes later, they walked into a room with white curtains and a single bed. In that bed was Jamie's mum, and in his mum's arms was a bundle of blankets.

"Come and meet your new sister, Jamie," said his mum. "She's just woken up."

20   Jamie hesitantly approached the bed as his mum lowered the bundle. Inside it, a tiny face was peering up at him.

"Mum!" he said before he could stop himself. "She's got the same colour eyes as me!"

"Do you want to hold her?" his mum asked.

Immediately, Jamie sat down on the bed, holding out his arms for his little sister.

Answer these questions about the text that you've just read. Circle the letter of the correct option for each question.

1. According to the text, why doesn't Jamie want a sister?

    A   He doesn't like other children.
    B   He's worried his sister will be better than he is at everything.
    C   He's not a competitive person.
    D   He thinks his parents will have less time for him.

2. Why does Jamie's grandma suggest that they buy some flowers for his mum?

   A   Jamie's mum needs flowers to decorate her hospital room.
   B   She's trying to make Jamie forget about his sister.
   C   She's as reluctant as Jamie is to meet his sister.
   D   She's trying to encourage Jamie to join in the celebration.

3. Which of the following best describes how Jamie feels about his sister at the end of the text?

   A   He's surprised that it took him so long to like his sister.
   B   He's fascinated by the similarity between himself and his sister.
   C   He's worried about his sister replacing him.
   D   He's angry that his sister looks like him.

4. What does the word "imminent" (line 11) mean in the context of the text?

   A   Commencing
   B   Foreseen
   C   Approaching
   D   Dreaded

Find the word that means the same, or nearly the same, as the word on the left. Underline your answer. Look at this example:

Example: rural   urban   <u>rustic</u>   quiet   wild

5. **seize**   presume   commandeer   ransack   control

6. **idolise**   follow   promote   worship   support

7. **ideal**   optimal   extreme   complete   promising

8. **trespass**   access   infringe   disregard   interfere

9. **moral**   accurate   commendable   judicious   righteous

10. **organic**   healthy   natural   bodily   agricultural

11. **skim**   glance   check   survey   scan

Mixed Practice Tests

Fill in the missing letters to complete the words in the following passage.

There are numerous languages spoken in the British Isles, one of which is Scottish Gaelic.

12. In the fourth and fifth centuries, settlers from Ireland [ ]n t[ ][ ]d u[ ]e[ ]

    their language, Gaelic, to the inhabitants of Scotland.

13. Gaelic [ ]v[ ]l[ ]e d over centuries into the language that is now known as

14. Scottish Gaelic and became [ ]i[ ]e[ ]p[ ]e[ ]d throughout the country.

    However, due to a series of conflicts between Scottish and English monarchs, the use of

15. Scottish Gaelic began to decline s[ ]e[ ]p[ ]y in the eleventh century.

    English eventually became the main language used in Scotland, and the

16. a u[ ][ ]o[ ]i t[ ][ ]s suppressed the use of Scottish Gaelic. Until the

17. mid-twentieth century, children could even be p[ ]n i[ ]h[ ][ ] for using the

    language at school. As a result, today there are only around 55 000 people who are

18. fluent in Scottish Gaelic. In r[ ]c[ ][ ]t years, however, the Scottish government

19. has attempted to r[ ]v[ ]v[ ] the language in Scotland. To encourage its use,

20. Scottish Gaelic has been made more v[ ]s[ ]b[ ][ ]. For example, many train

21. stations and roads have bilingual signs. A number of schools now [ ]f[ ][ ]r

    teaching in both English and Scottish Gaelic so that children grow up with an

22. [ ]p[ ]r e[ ]i a[ ]o n of both languages. Furthermore, some

23. television channels and radio stations b[ ][ ][ ]d c a[ ][ ] in Scottish Gaelic,

    and new Scottish Gaelic literature is being published.

24. The government's [ ]b[ ][ ]c t[ ]v e is to increase the number of Scottish

25. Gaelic [ ]p[ ]a k[ ][ ]s and prevent the language from becoming extinct.

Total (out of 25): [ ]

CGP

There are **multiple-choice answer sheets** for these questions on our website —
go to www.cgpbooks.co.uk/11plusanswersheets. If you want to attempt each test-style
paper more than once, you will need to print a separate answer sheet for each attempt.
If you'd prefer to answer the questions in write-in format, write directly on the test.

11+ Test-Style Paper 1
For Ages 10-11
Verbal Reasoning
For the CEM Test

Read the following:

Do not start the test until you are told to do so.

1. This test can be taken in either multiple-choice or write-in format.

2. If you are taking it as a multiple-choice test, you should mark your answer to each question
   in pencil on the answer sheet you've printed from www.cgpbooks.co.uk/11plusanswersheets.
   Mark the correct box quickly and neatly using a horizontal line.

3. If you are taking it as a write-in test, you should write your answer to each question in
   pencil on the paper. Write your answer carefully in the space provided or, if there is a
   range of options, mark the correct box quickly and neatly using a horizontal line.

4. If you make a mistake, rub it out and mark your new answer clearly.

5. There are five sections in this test.

6. The time allowed for each section is given at the start of that section.
   You will have a total of 30 minutes to complete the timed sections of the test.

7. Each section includes examples showing you how to answer the questions.
   You may refer to these examples at any time as you work through the section.

8. Do as many questions as you can. For some questions you will be given a range of options
   — if you get stuck on one of these questions, choose the answer that you think is most likely
   to be correct, then move on to the next question. If you get stuck on a question for which
   no options are given, leave it and move on to the next question. If you have time at the
   end of the section, go back and have another go at the questions you could not answer.

9. You should do any rough working on a separate piece of paper.

Work carefully, but go as quickly as you can.

Section 1: Comprehension

Example Read these example questions. You may return to these examples at any time as you work through this section.

The Houses of Parliament

1   The Houses of Parliament are made up of the House of Commons and the House of
Lords. Collectively, they are also known as the Palace of Westminster. Located in the centre
of London on the banks of the River Thames, these Gothic buildings are where laws are
discussed and voted on. Debates take place in special chambers, which are designed so
5   that the opposing sides can sit in long rows across from each other. The buildings date back
hundreds of years to the time of the Anglo-Saxons, when members of royalty lived in palaces
nearby and had a more active role in legal decision-making than modern royalty.

The Houses of Parliament have a chequered history and have been the location of many
significant events. One of the most infamous of these events occurred in 1605, when a plot
10   to blow up the Houses of Parliament was foiled. The perpetrators were caught and eventually
executed. The occasion is marked in the UK by Guy Fawkes' Night every 5th November.
More than two hundred years later in 1834, a devastating fire struck the Houses of Parliament.
Extensive rebuilding work had to be carried out, and the buildings have looked much the same
to this day.

(A) According to the text, which of the following statements
about the Houses of Parliament is false?

- [ ] A   Anglo-Saxon palaces were once located nearby.
- [▬] B   They look the same as they did in Anglo-Saxon times.
- [ ] C   They were nearly damaged by explosives.
- [ ] D   Debates are held inside.

(B) A plot to destroy the Houses of Parliament was "foiled" (line 10). This means:

- [ ] A   The plot was discovered just before it was carried out.
- [ ] B   The plot came as a surprise to everyone.
- [▬] C   The plot was prevented from going ahead.
- [ ] D   The plot wasn't clever enough to be successful.

End of example questions

Go to the next page ➡

There are 16 questions in this section

Read the passage carefully and then answer the questions that follow.

An adapted extract from 'Little Men'

1   "Please, sir, is this Plumfield?" asked a ragged boy of the man who opened the great gate.
     "Yes. Who sent you?"
     "Mr Laurence. I have got a letter for the lady."
     "All right; go up to the house, and give it to her; she'll see to you, little chap."

5   The man spoke pleasantly, and the boy went on, feeling much cheered by the words.
Through the soft spring rain that fell on sprouting grass and budding trees, Nat saw a large
square house before him, a hospitable-looking house, with an old-fashioned porch, wide steps,
and lights shining in many windows. Neither curtains nor shutters hid the cheerful glimmer; and,
pausing a moment before he rang, Nat saw many little shadows dancing on the walls, heard the

10   pleasant hum of young voices, and felt that it was hardly possible that the light and warmth and
comfort within could be for a homeless "little chap" like him.
     "I hope the lady will see to me," he thought, and gave a timid rap with the great bronze
knocker, which was a jovial griffin's head.
     A rosy-faced servant-maid opened the door, and smiled as she took the letter which he

15   silently offered. She seemed used to receiving strange boys, for she pointed to a seat in the hall:
     "Sit there and drip on the mat a bit, while I take this in to missis."
     Nat found plenty to amuse him while he waited, and stared about him curiously, enjoying the
view, yet glad to do so unobserved in the dusky recess by the door.
     The house seemed swarming with boys, who were beguiling the rainy twilight with all sorts of

20   amusements. There were boys everywhere, apparently, for various open doors showed pleasant
groups of big boys, little boys, and middle-sized boys in all stages of evening relaxation, not
to say liveliness. Two large rooms on the right were evidently schoolrooms, for desks, maps,
blackboards and books were scattered about. An open fire burned on the hearth, and several
indolent lads lay on their backs before it, discussing a new cricket ground, with such animation

25   that their boots waved in the air. A tall youth was practising on the flute in one corner, quite
undisturbed by the racket all about him. Two or three others were jumping over the desks,
pausing, now and then, to get their breath and laugh at the amusing sketches of a little wag* who
was caricaturing the whole household on a blackboard.
     In the room on the left a long supper-table was seen, set forth with great pitchers of new milk,

30   piles of brown and white bread, and perfect stacks of shiny gingerbread. A flavour of toast was
in the air, also hints of baked apples, very tantalising to one hungry little nose and stomach.

The hall, however, presented the most inviting prospect of all, for a brisk game of tag was going on in the upper entry. One landing was devoted to marbles, the other to checkers**, while the stairs were occupied by a boy reading, a girl singing a lullaby to her doll, two puppies, a kitten

35 and a constant succession of small boys sliding down the banisters, to the great detriment of their clothes and danger to their limbs.

So absorbed did Nat become in this exciting race, that he ventured farther and farther out of his corner. One very lively boy came down so swiftly that he could not stop himself, and fell off the banisters with a crash that would have broken any head but one rendered nearly as hard as

40 a cannon-ball by eleven years of constant bumping. Nat forgot himself, and ran up to the fallen rider, expecting to find him half-dead. The boy, however, only winked rapidly for a second, then lay calmly looking up at the new face with a surprised, "Hullo!"

"Hullo!" returned Nat, not knowing what else to say, and thinking that reply brief and easy.

"Are you a new boy?" asked the recumbent youth, without stirring.

45 "Don't know yet."

"What's your name?"

"Nat Blake."

"Mine's Tommy Bangs. Come up and have a go, will you?" and Tommy got up on his legs like one suddenly remembering the duties of hospitality.

50 "Guess I won't, till I see whether I'm going to stay or not," returned Nat, feeling the desire to stay increase every moment.

"I say, Demi, here's a new one. Come and say hello," and the lively Thomas returned to his sport with unabated relish.

At his call, the boy reading on the stairs looked up with big brown eyes, and after an instant's

55 pause, as if a little shy, he put the book under his arm, and came soberly to greet the newcomer, who found something very attractive in the pleasant face of this slender, mild-eyed boy.

"Have you seen Aunt Jo?" he asked, as if that was some sort of important ceremony.

"I haven't seen anybody yet but you boys; I'm waiting," answered Nat.

"Did Uncle Laurie send you?" proceeded Demi, politely, but gravely.

60 "Mr Laurence did."

"He is Uncle Laurie; and he always sends nice boys."

Nat looked gratified at the remark, and smiled, in a way that made his thin face very pleasant. He did not know what to say next, so the two stood staring at one another in friendly silence.

by Louisa May Alcott

* wag — *joker*
** *checkers — a board game, also known as draughts*

Answer these questions about the text. You can refer back to the text if you need to.
Pick the best answer and draw a line through the rectangle next to it.

(1) According to the text, which of the following statements about the house must be false?

- ☐ **A**   The house is very old.
- ☐ **B**   The house is surrounded by gardens.
- ☐ **C**   The house looks intimidating.
- ☐ **D**   The house has three storeys.

(2) Which of the following best describes how Nat feels in lines 1-13?

- ☐ **A**   Confident and enthusiastic
- ☐ **B**   Discouraged and intimidated
- ☐ **C**   Confused but intrigued
- ☐ **D**   Hopeful but uncertain

(3) Which of the following statements is true?

- ☐ **A**   The servant-maid doesn't find Nat's arrival at the house unusual.
- ☐ **B**   The man at the gate warned the servant-maid that Nat was coming.
- ☐ **C**   The servant-maid received a letter to tell her Nat was coming.
- ☐ **D**   The staff were expecting Nat to arrive at the house.

(4) Why does the servant-maid ask Nat to sit down in line 16?

1) To give Nat a chance to rest after his journey.
2) So he can dry off.
3) To give Nat time to get used to the house.
4) She wants Nat to wait while she finds the lady of the house.

- ☐ **A**   1 and 3
- ☐ **B**   3 and 4
- ☐ **C**   2 and 4
- ☐ **D**   2 and 3

(5) "The house seemed swarming with boys" (line 19).
What does this mean?

- ☐ **A**   The house is crowded with boys.
- ☐ **B**   The boys are very messy.
- ☐ **C**   The boys are all grouped together in one room.
- ☐ **D**   The boys are making lots of noise.

6 What time of day is it when Nat arrives at the house?

- ☐ **A** Morning
- ☐ **B** Midday
- ☐ **C** Afternoon
- ☐ **D** Evening

7 According to the text, which of the following are the children in the house not doing?

- ☐ **A** Eating
- ☐ **B** Singing
- ☐ **C** Drawing
- ☐ **D** Playing games

8 The narrator states that the hall "presented the most inviting prospect of all" (line 32). What does this mean?

- ☐ **A** Nat feels lucky to have seen the hall.
- ☐ **B** The hall is the only interesting room in the house.
- ☐ **C** Nat is more interested by what is in the hall than by anything else.
- ☐ **D** There is a nice view from the hall window.

9 Which of the following statements about Tommy cannot be true?

- ☐ **A** He has hit his head multiple times.
- ☐ **B** He is ten years old.
- ☐ **C** He has been at Plumfield for eleven years.
- ☐ **D** He is responsible for supervising the other boys.

10 Which of the following best describes Tommy?

- ☐ **A** Arrogant
- ☐ **B** Welcoming
- ☐ **C** Forgetful
- ☐ **D** Patient

Go to the next question ⇨

(11) Why doesn't Nat join Tommy in sliding down the banister?

    ☐ **A**   He doesn't want to get hurt.
    ☐ **B**   He is too shy to join in.
    ☐ **C**   He wants to make a good first impression.
    ☐ **D**   He wants to wait and see if he will be allowed to stay first.

(12) Which of the following is not mentioned in the text?

    ☐ **A**   Why Nat needs to see the lady of house.
    ☐ **B**   Who sent Nat to Plumfield.
    ☐ **C**   Whether Nat stays at Plumfield.
    ☐ **D**   What Nat's surname is.

(13) What does the word "tantalising" (line 31) mean?

    ☐ **A**   Pleasant
    ☐ **B**   Delicious
    ☐ **C**   Tempting
    ☐ **D**   Frustrating

(14) What does the word "detriment" (line 35) mean in the context of the text?

    ☐ **A**   Suffering
    ☐ **B**   Damage
    ☐ **C**   Prejudice
    ☐ **D**   Disintegration

(15) What is meant by the phrase "unabated relish" (line 53)?

    ☐ **A**   Increased recklessness
    ☐ **B**   Unmistakable embarrassment
    ☐ **C**   Undiminished enjoyment
    ☐ **D**   Extreme caution

(16) What does the word "soberly" (line 55) mean?

    ☐ **A**   Slowly and moodily
    ☐ **B**   Quietly and seriously
    ☐ **C**   Sympathetically and kindly
    ☐ **D**   Helpfully and quickly

Section 2: Shuffled Sentences

Example	Read this example question. You may return to this example at any time as you work through this section.

Rearrange the words so that each sentence makes sense.
Mark the rectangle under the word which does **not** fit into the sentence.

A ticket   a   train   bought   did   he
   ☐   ☐   ☐   ☐   ▬   ☐

The remaining words can be rearranged to make the sentence: 'He bought a train ticket.'

You have 4 minutes to complete this section

There are 8 questions in this section

Rearrange the words so that each sentence makes sense.
Mark the rectangle under the word which does **not** fit into the sentence.

17 a   the   for   we   to   sit   went   park   picnic
   ☐   ☐   ☐   ☐   ☐   ☐   ☐   ☐   ☐

18 could   not   plant   without   the   lack   water   enough   grow
   ☐   ☐   ☐   ☐   ☐   ☐   ☐   ☐   ☐

19 joining   team   about   football   for   hard   Suzie   new   a   thought
   ☐   ☐   ☐   ☐   ☐   ☐   ☐   ☐   ☐   ☐

20 remember   your   to   their   neighbour   give   post   write
   ☐   ☐   ☐   ☐   ☐   ☐   ☐   ☐

21 dog   the   run   squirrel   to   began   chase   a
   ☐   ☐   ☐   ☐   ☐   ☐   ☐   ☐

22 to   Arthur   failed   last   evenings   lock   window   the   night
   ☐   ☐   ☐   ☐   ☐   ☐   ☐   ☐   ☐

23 got   to   journey   took   the   her   surfer   the   seaside   on   lost
   ☐   ☐   ☐   ☐   ☐   ☐   ☐   ☐   ☐   ☐   ☐

24 bite   slices   this   cake   a   try   chocolate   of
   ☐   ☐   ☐   ☐   ☐   ☐   ☐   ☐

Test-Style Paper 1

Section 3: Synonyms

Example Read this example question. You may return to this example at any time as you work through this section.

Choose the word which means the same, or nearly the same, as the word on the left.

(A) **still**   motionless   lazy   listless   idle
                ▬   ☐   ☐   ☐

⏱ You have 4 minutes to complete this section ⏱

There are 10 questions in this section

Choose the word which means the same, or nearly the same, as the word on the left.

(25) **prove**   assert   accept   validate   outline
               ☐   ☐   ☐   ☐

(26) **stranded**   forgotten   neglected   expelled   marooned
               ☐   ☐   ☐   ☐

(27) **saga**   edition   era   essay   story
               ☐   ☐   ☐   ☐

(28) **entitled**   equipped   awarded   justified   permitted
               ☐   ☐   ☐   ☐

(29) **prone**   agreeable   liable   favourable   impressionable
               ☐   ☐   ☐   ☐

(30) **attract**   lure   ensnare   beckon   compel
               ☐   ☐   ☐   ☐

(31) **adorned**   embellished   enhanced   detailed   colourful
               ☐   ☐   ☐   ☐

(32) **collection**   acquisition   pairing   package   assemblage
               ☐   ☐   ☐   ☐

(33) **inferior**   subordinate   superior   servile   shorter
               ☐   ☐   ☐   ☐

(34) **apply**   advise   implement   perform   attempt
               ☐   ☐   ☐   ☐

Section 4: Antonyms

Example Read this example question. You may return to this example at any time as you work through this section.

Complete the word on the right so that it means the opposite, or nearly the opposite, of the word on the left.

(A) brighten | f | a | d | e |

You have 4 minutes to complete this section

There are 10 questions in this section

Complete the word on the right so that it means the opposite, or nearly the opposite, of the word on the left.

(35) injure | | e | a | |

(36) misapprehend | | n | | | r | s | | a | n | |

(37) evil | v | | r | | | o | u | |

(38) concur | q | | | r | | | | l |

(39) friendly | | o | s | t | | | l | |

(40) faith | m | | s | | r | | s | |

(41) fair | | n | | u | s | |

(42) strict | | e | l | a | | | d |

(43) phenomenal | o | | | i | | a | | y |

(44) deceptive | | o | n | | s | |

Test-Style Paper 1

Section 5: Cloze

Example Read these example questions. You may return to these examples at any time as you work through this section.

Millions of years ago, dinosaurs (A) ☐ soared ☐ predated ■ roamed ☐ hunted the Earth. To this day, scientists are

(B) ☐ recognising ■ unearthing ☐ noticing ☐ burying the fossils of dinosaurs that were previously not known to exist.

You have 6 minutes to complete this section

(45) ☐ Obvious ☐ Common ☐ Famed ☐ Definite for its towering walls of red rock, the Grand Canyon is one of the

world's best-known landmarks. Located in the United States, the canyon (46) ☐ extends ☐ develops ☐ projects ☐ elongates

for 277 miles, and is a mile deep in some places. The area (47) ☐ attends ☐ draws ☐ pulls ☐ frequents a huge

number of tourists, who come from all around the world to view this (48) ☐ gratifying ☐ astonishing ☐ ludicrous ☐ alarming

desert landscape. Visitors even come in the winter, when temperatures (49) ☐ arise ☐ stabilise ☐ plummet ☐ hurtle

and snow lines the cliffs. The canyon also has an (50) ☐ extensive ☐ ageless ☐ sizeable ☐ longing history — over time, the powerful Colorado River has cut down through the rock, exposing distinct layers

51
☐ beneath
☐ amidst
☐ along
☐ near

the length of the canyon (making it easy for scientists to study them).

The oldest layer of exposed rock is around two billion years old,

52
☐ until
☐ since
☐ except
☐ while

the

youngest layer is

53
☐ hardly
☐ fairly
☐ even
☐ only

around 100 000 years old. At the bottom of the canyon,

the river

54
☐ splits
☐ winds
☐ follows
☐ shifts

its way between the cliffs. Many people

55
☐ enjoy
☐ practise
☐ strive
☐ partake

in

river rafting experiences and brave the river in inflatable rafts. Additionally, walking trails

provide

56
☐ multitude
☐ numerous
☐ hundreds
☐ plenty

opportunities

57
☐ at
☐ for
☐ in
☐ by

sightseeing. However, hikers

need to be

58
☐ insightful
☐ vigilant
☐ receptive
☐ secretive

, as there are creatures that may

59
☐ pose
☐ state
☐ deliver
☐ cause

a threat,

such as rattlesnakes that

60
☐ conceal
☐ disguise
☐ hide
☐ blend

into the surrounding rock.

This is the end of the test.

CGP

11+ Test-Style Paper 2
For Ages 10-11
Verbal Reasoning
For the CEM Test

Read the following:

Do not start the test until you are told to do so.

1. This test can be taken in either multiple-choice or write-in format.

2. If you are taking it as a multiple-choice test, you should mark your answer to each question in pencil on the answer sheet you've printed from www.cgpbooks.co.uk/11plusanswersheets. Mark the correct box quickly and neatly using a horizontal line.

3. If you are taking it as a write-in test, you should write your answer to each question in pencil on the paper. Write your answer carefully in the space provided or, if there is a range of options, mark the correct box quickly and neatly using a horizontal line.

4. If you make a mistake, rub it out and mark your new answer clearly.

5. There are six sections in this test.

6. The time allowed for each section is given at the start of that section. You will have a total of 30 minutes to complete the timed sections of the test.

7. Each section includes examples showing you how to answer the questions. You may refer to these examples at any time as you work through the section.

8. Do as many questions as you can. For some questions you will be given a range of options — if you get stuck on one of these questions, choose the answer that you think is most likely to be correct, then move on to the next question. If you get stuck on a question for which no options are given, leave it and move on to the next question. If you have time at the end of the section, go back and have another go at the questions you could not answer.

9. You should do any rough working on a separate piece of paper.

Work carefully, but go as quickly as you can.

Section 1: Comprehension

Example Read these example questions. You may return to these examples at any time as you work through this section.

The Houses of Parliament

1   The Houses of Parliament are made up of the House of Commons and the House of Lords. Collectively, they are also known as the Palace of Westminster. Located in the centre of London on the banks of the River Thames, these Gothic buildings are where laws are discussed and voted on. Debates take place in special chambers, which are designed so

5   that the opposing sides can sit in long rows across from each other. The buildings date back hundreds of years to the time of the Anglo-Saxons, when members of royalty lived in palaces nearby and had a more active role in legal decision-making than modern royalty.

The Houses of Parliament have a chequered history and have been the location of many significant events. One of the most infamous of these events occurred in 1605, when a plot

10   to blow up the Houses of Parliament was foiled. The perpetrators were caught and eventually executed. The occasion is marked in the UK by Guy Fawkes' Night every 5th November. More than two hundred years later in 1834, a devastating fire struck the Houses of Parliament. Extensive rebuilding work had to be carried out, and the buildings have looked much the same to this day.

(A) According to the text, which of the following statements about the Houses of Parliament is false?

- ☐ **A** Anglo-Saxon palaces were once located nearby.
- ▬ **B** They look the same as they did in Anglo-Saxon times.
- ☐ **C** They were nearly damaged by explosives.
- ☐ **D** Debates are held inside.

(B) A plot to destroy the Houses of Parliament was "foiled" (line 10). This means:

- ☐ **A** The plot was discovered just before it was carried out.
- ☐ **B** The plot came as a surprise to everyone.
- ▬ **C** The plot was prevented from going ahead.
- ☐ **D** The plot wasn't clever enough to be successful.

End of example questions

Go to the next page ⇨

⏱ You have 8 minutes to complete this section ⏱

There are 8 questions in this section

Read the passage carefully and then answer the questions that follow.

El Dorado

1   The legend of El Dorado has fascinated people from all over the world for over five hundred
years. Perhaps the best-known version of this myth describes El Dorado as an ancient city
made of gold, hidden somewhere in South America. However, if you trace the story back to its
origins, El Dorado was not a city at all.

5   Spanish explorers first heard the tale of El Dorado when they arrived in South America in
the early 1500s. The details of the original story vary, but one version spoke of a tribal chief
who was seen covering himself in gold dust from head to toe. Because of his supposed
penchant for gold, the Spanish explorers gave this chief his now legendary title 'El Dorado',
which translates to "The Golden One".

10   The explorers' imaginations ran wild, and the story of El Dorado was embellished with every
retelling. Eventually, El Dorado was transformed from one rich man into an entire golden city,
overflowing with riches beyond anyone's wildest dreams.

The prospect of immeasurable wealth was so enthralling that people from across the globe
came searching for this fabled city. In the 1550s, Spanish explorers heard of a lake high in

15   the Andes mountains called Lake Guatavita that was supposedly filled with gold. Believing it
to be somehow connected to the lost city of El Dorado, multiple attempts were made over the
years to drain the lake and pillage the riches that lay in its depths. As the water levels fell, vast
quantities of gold were revealed around the periphery of the lake. However, they were unable
to drain the lake entirely, and the treasures that lay at the bottom of it remained a mystery.

20   While the city of El Dorado may be no more than a tantalising story fabricated by
over-imaginative explorers, there is evidence to suggest that 'The Golden One' was more than
just a myth. In 1636, a writer called Juan Rodriguez Freyle described a ceremony carried out
by the Muisca people which bore a curious similarity to the story of the golden chief heard
by the Spanish explorers a hundred years earlier, and also explained the presence of gold in

25   Lake Guatavita.

The Muisca people were one of the most advanced ancient civilisations of the Americas
(alongside others such as the Inca and the Maya). According to Freyle, when one Muisca
leader died, a public ceremony took place to initiate his successor. Accompanied by four high
priests, the new leader would cover himself in gold dust and sail out to the middle of a sacred

30   lake, such as Lake Guatavita, on a raft laden with precious objects. The gilded chief would
then cast golden statues, known as *tunjos*, and other treasures into the centre of the lake as
offerings to help him commune with the deities.

Some three hundred years after Freyle described the Muisca ceremony, a golden statue
of a raft was discovered in a small cave in Colombia, depicting a scene almost identical to
35 Freyle's account of the chief and his four high priests. It is now known as the Muisca Raft, and
is on display in the Gold Museum in Colombia's capital city of Bogota. While no evidence of
a lost city has ever been found, this artefact supports Freyle's account and suggests that the
story of El Dorado does have its basis in real events.

Much has changed since the 1500s, but one thing that remains the same is the universal
40 obsession with gold. To this day, looters still plunder the area around Lake Guatavita,
searching for golden artefacts to melt down for money. This has undoubtedly led to the loss of
irreplaceable relics that could have given great insight into the civilisation that inspired one of
the most famous and enduring legends of ancient America.

Go to the next page

Answer these questions about the text. You can refer back to the text if you need to.
Pick the best answer and draw a line through the rectangle next to it.

(1) According to the text, why did Spanish explorers name the tribal chief 'El Dorado'?

    ☐ **A**   Because they were impressed by his wealth.
    ☐ **B**   Because he was the richest man in South America.
    ☐ **C**   Because he covered himself in gold.
    ☐ **D**   Because they wanted him to become famous around the world.

(2) "The story of El Dorado was embellished with every retelling" (lines 10-11). This means:

    ☐ **A**   people discovered more facts about El Dorado.
    ☐ **B**   the story was retold by thousands of people.
    ☐ **C**   the story became more famous over time.
    ☐ **D**   new details were added to the story each time it was told.

(3) According to the text, why is the account written by Juan Rodriguez Freyle significant?

1) It explains why gold was discovered in Lake Guatavita.
2) It proves that explorers shared tales of a city made of gold.
3) It suggests that the story of 'The Golden One' was based on real events.
4) It has encouraged people to search for gold in South America.

    ☐ **A**   1 and 3
    ☐ **B**   1 and 4
    ☐ **C**   2 and 4
    ☐ **D**   3 and 4

(4) Which of the following statements must be true?

    ☐ **A**   By 1600, people had stopped looking for the lost city of gold.
    ☐ **B**   Not all *tunjos* were made of gold.
    ☐ **C**   The Muisca people found Lake Guatavita in the 1550s.
    ☐ **D**   The Muisca Raft was discovered in the 1900s.

(5) According to the text, which of the following statements must be false?

    ☐ **A**   The Muisca Raft was found in a cave.
    ☐ **B**   The Muisca were one of only three ancient civilisations in the Americas.
    ☐ **C**   Juan Rodriguez Freyle was born in the late 1500s.
    ☐ **D**   There is undiscovered gold at the bottom of Lake Guatavita.

Section 2: Synonyms

Example Read this example question. You may return to this example at any time as you work through this section.

Complete the word on the right so that it means the same, or nearly the same, as the word on the left.

(A) unkind   c r u e l

---

4 **You have 4 minutes to complete this section** **4**

There are 10 questions in this section

Complete the word on the right so that it means the same, or nearly the same, as the word on the left.

(9) consume   d ☐ v ☐ ☐ r

(10) forge   ☐ ☐ l s ☐ f y

(11) mutual   s ☐ ☐ r ☐ d

(12) manner   d e ☐ e ☐ ☐ o u ☐

(13) obedient   ☐ o m ☐ ☐ i ☐ n t

(14) permit   ☐ ☐ t ☐ o r ☐ s e

(15) complicated   c ☐ ☐ v ☐ l ☐ ☐ e d

(16) admired   ☐ s ☐ e ☐ m e ☐

(17) seriousness   g r ☐ ☐ i ☐ y

(18) discern   ☐ e ☐ o g ☐ i s ☐

Section 3: Antonyms

Example Read this example question. You may return to this example at any time as you work through this section.

Choose the word which means the opposite, or nearly the opposite, of the word on the left.

(A) **agitated**   serene   tired   silent   satisfied
              ▬   ☐   ☐   ☐

⏱ 4 You have 4 minutes to complete this section ⏱ 4

There are 10 questions in this section

Choose the word which means the opposite, or nearly the opposite, of the word on the left.

(19) **concede**   deny   avert   recede   exceed
                ☐   ☐   ☐   ☐

(20) **liberate**   lock   ransom   prevent   detain
                ☐   ☐   ☐   ☐

(21) **active**   reluctant   muted   stagnant   faltering
                ☐   ☐   ☐   ☐

(22) **insensitivity**   tact   certainty   tolerance   wisdom
                      ☐   ☐   ☐   ☐

(23) **provoke**   appease   attract   justify   apologise
                 ☐   ☐   ☐   ☐

(24) **improve**   negate   degenerate   confine   expire
                ☐.   ☐   ☐   ☐

(25) **noticeable**   suggestible   distant   faded   imperceptible
                     ☐   ☐   ☐   ☐

(26) **destructive**   cautious   peaceful   agreeable   beneficial
                     ☐   ☐   ☐   ☐

(27) **ignorance**   understanding   interest   educating   maturity
                    ☐   ☐   ☐   ☐

(28) **honesty**   ingenuity   duplicity   inability   apathy
                ☐   ☐   ☐   ☐

Test-Style Paper 2

Section 4: Multiple Meanings

Example Read this example question. You may return to this example at any time as you work through this section.

Choose the word which has a similar meaning to the words in both sets of brackets.

(A) (blaze flame) (scorch char)   fire flare burn toast
    ☐   ☐   ▬   ☐

⏱ You have **4** minutes to complete this section ⏱

There are 8 questions in this section

Choose the word which has a similar meaning to the words in both sets of brackets.

(29) (discuss consult) (grant bestow)   debate confer award review
    ☐   ☐   ☐   ☐

(30) (method mode) (intends plans)   ways tactics means attempts
    ☐   ☐   ☐   ☐

(31) (ponder consider) (intentional meant)   ponder muse wilful deliberate
    ☐   ☐   ☐   ☐

(32) (different unalike) (clear plain)   distinct unique obvious discrete
    ☐   ☐   ☐   ☐

(33) (observe watch) (respect approval)   view honour regard behold
    ☐   ☐   ☐   ☐

(34) (proceed continue) (headway advance)   travel persist rise progress
    ☐   ☐   ☐   ☐

(35) (unnerve unsettle) (interrupt bother)   petrify disturb alarm harass
    ☐   ☐   ☐   ☐

(36) (sever detach) (distant apart)   isolated break separate damage
    ☐   ☐   ☐   ☐

Section 5: Odd One Out

Example **Read this example question. You may return to this example at any time as you work through this section.**

Three of the words in each list are linked.
Mark the rectangle under the word that is **not** related to these three.

(A) friend   companion   enemy   playmate
    ☐   ☐   ▬   ☐

(4) You have 4 minutes to complete this section (4)

There are 10 questions in this section

Three of the words in each list are linked.
Mark the rectangle under the word that is **not** related to these three.

(37) cultivate   harvest   nurture   tend
     ☐   ☐   ☐   ☐

(38) appalled   horrified   bewildered   dismayed
     ☐   ☐   ☐   ☐

(39) praise   compliment   commend   please
     ☐   ☐   ☐   ☐

(40) truck   trailer   car   van
     ☐   ☐   ☐   ☐

(41) dent   hollow   cavity   knoll
     ☐   ☐   ☐   ☐

(42) crops   wheat   oats   barley
     ☐   ☐   ☐   ☐

(43) feathers   scales   fabric   fur
     ☐   ☐   ☐   ☐

(44) mustard   marmalade   ketchup   mayonnaise
     ☐   ☐   ☐   ☐

(45) satisfied   fulfilled   saturated   gratified
     ☐   ☐   ☐   ☐

(46) rainstorm   tide   downpour   deluge
     ☐   ☐   ☐   ☐

Section 6: Cloze

Example Read these example questions. You may return to these examples at any time as you work through this section.

(A) When decorating a Christmas tree, many people start by h a n g i n g

up the lights, distributing them as evenly as possible from the top to the bottom.

(B) They then fill any available space between the lights with b a u b l e s,

(C) making sure to place their f a v o u r i t e s at the front.

⏱ 6 You have 6 minutes to complete this section ⏱ 6

There are 14 questions in this section

Fill in the missing letters to complete the words in the following passage.

(47) When you ☐ o n ☐ i ☐ ☐ r getting a new pet, your mind probably

jumps immediately to a dog, a cat, or perhaps a hamster. Not many people would

(48) c ☐ n ☐ e ☐ p ☐ a ☐ e the possibility of a pet rat, perhaps due to

(49) the s ☐ e ☐ e ☐ t y ☐ e that they inhabit dark, dirty places.

(50) However, domesticated rats d ☐ ☐ f ☐ r from their sewer-dwelling

cousins in a variety of ways. Many pet rats are a breed known as 'fancy rats',

and they are smaller in size than wild brown rats, with bigger ears and longer tails.

(51) Fancy rats are naturally ☐ n q ☐ i s ☐ t ☐ v ☐, clean and

(52) easily trained. They can be taught to ☐ e r ☐ ☐ r ☐ tricks, ranging

(53) from ☐ b ☐ y ☐ n g simple commands, such as 'stand up' and

(54) 'turn around', to solving i ☐ t ☐ ☐ c a ☐ e puzzles.

Section 6: Cloze

(55) As long as there is a reward at stake, fancy rats will u☐☐l☐se

(56) all the skills at their disposal to acquire it. Their ☐ne☐g☐☐ic

nature, loyalty and love of playing games, such as tug of war, causes some

(57) people to ☐☐k☐n them to tiny dogs.

Fancy rats are also incredibly sociable animals, which makes them affectionate

(58) and engaging c☐☐p☐n☐☐ns for children and adults alike.

(59) Human i☐t☐r☐a☐t☐☐n alone isn't enough for these furry

little socialites, however. They should always be kept in same-sex pairs or

(60) small groups to prevent ☐☐n☐l☐n☐ss.

This is the end of the test.

Glossary

adjective	A word that <u>describes</u> a <u>noun</u>, e.g. '<u>beautiful</u> morning', '<u>frosty</u> lawn'.
adverb	A word that <u>describes</u> a <u>verb</u> or an <u>adjective</u>, which often ends with the <u>suffix</u> '<u>-ly</u>', e.g. 'She laughed <u>happily</u>.', 'He ran <u>quickly</u>.'
antonym	A word that has the <u>opposite meaning</u> to another word, e.g. the antonym of '<u>good</u>' is '<u>bad</u>'.
conjunction	A word or phrase that <u>joins</u> two clauses, e.g. '<u>and</u>', '<u>but</u>'.
consonants	The <u>21 letters</u> of the alphabet that <u>aren't vowels</u>.
fiction	Text that has been <u>made up</u> by the author, about <u>imaginary people</u> and <u>events</u>.
homographs	Words that are spelt the same but have <u>different meanings</u>, e.g. 'I want to <u>play</u>.' and 'I saw a <u>play</u>.'
homophones	Words that <u>sound the same</u>, but mean different things, e.g. '<u>hair</u>' and '<u>hare</u>'.
imagery	Language that creates a <u>vivid picture</u> in the reader's mind.
metaphor	A way of <u>describing</u> something by saying that it <u>is</u> something else, e.g. 'John's legs were lead weights.'
multiple choice	A type of <u>11+ question</u> that gives you <u>answers</u> to choose from.
non-fiction	Text that is about <u>facts</u> and <u>real people</u> and <u>events</u>.
noun	A word that <u>names</u> something, e.g. '<u>Paul</u>', '<u>cat</u>', '<u>fear</u>', '<u>childhood</u>'.
personification	A way of describing something by giving it <u>human feelings</u> and <u>characteristics</u>, e.g. 'The cruel wind plucked remorselessly at my threadbare clothes.'
prefix	A string of letters that can be put <u>in front</u> of a word to <u>change its meaning</u>, e.g. '<u>un-</u>' can be added to '<u>lock</u>' to make '<u>unlock</u>'.
pronoun	A word that can be used <u>instead</u> of a <u>noun</u>, e.g. '<u>I</u>', '<u>you</u>', '<u>he</u>', '<u>it</u>'.
simile	A way of describing something by <u>comparing</u> it to something else, e.g. 'The stars were <u>like</u> a thousand diamonds, glittering in the sky.'
subject	The <u>person</u> or <u>thing</u> doing the <u>action</u> of a verb, e.g. '<u>Jo</u> laughed.', '<u>The bird</u> flew.'
suffix	A string of letters that can be put <u>after</u> a word to <u>change its meaning</u>, e.g. '<u>-er</u>' can be added to the end of '<u>play</u>' to make '<u>player</u>'.
synonym	A word with a <u>similar meaning</u> to another word, e.g. '<u>big</u>' is a synonym of '<u>huge</u>'.
verb	An <u>action</u> or <u>doing</u> word, e.g. '<u>run</u>', '<u>went</u>', '<u>think</u>', or a <u>being</u> word, e.g. '<u>is</u>'.
vowels	The letters '<u>a</u>', '<u>e</u>', '<u>i</u>', '<u>o</u>' and '<u>u</u>'.

Answers

Section One — Spelling

Pages 4-5 — Preparing for the Test

1 Various answers possible, e.g. 'de-', 'ex-', 'mis-', 'post-' and 'pre-'.
These aren't the only possible answers. If you've got a different answer, you can check it in a dictionary.

2 a) Various answers possible, e.g. 'stroke', 'string', 'strict', 'stripe'.
   b) No. There are no words in English which begin with 'blr'.
   c) Various answers possible, e.g. 'shrink', 'shrub', 'shrug', 'shrine'.
   d) No. There are no words in English which begin with 'ds'.
Some combinations of letters never appear in English.

3 a) anywhere
   b) stubborn
   c) hovercraft
   d) shipwreck
These are the correct spellings of these words.

4 a) unnatural
   b) angrily
   c) misspell
   d) vaccinate
If a word ends in a vowel or a 'y', you'll usually have to take the last letter off before adding the suffix. If the word ends in a vowel followed by a 'y', you don't take off the last letter.

Pages 6-7 — Plurals

1 a) The plural of 'branch' is 'branches'.
   b) The plural of 'tooth' is 'teeth'.
   c) The plural of 'Grady' is 'Gradys'.
   d) The plural of 'wolf' is 'wolves'.
   e) The plural of 'dress' is 'dresses'.
Words ending with 'ch' or 's' usually take an 'es' plural, and words ending with 'y' usually take an 'ies' plural unless they are proper nouns.

Pages 8-9 — Homophones and Homographs

1 I'm supposed to go to drama group every Monday **night**, but this **week** I'm too tired. I've had a very busy day at school and I'm not feeling **great**. Instead, I think I'm going to stay **here** and watch a film that I haven't **seen** before.
The words in bold are the correct homophones.

2 a) Make sure that you know **where** you are going.
   b) Watch out for the crab — it has very sharp **claws**.
   c) At the theme park, we **rode** on four different roller coasters.
   d) The jockey pulled on the **reins** to get the horse to stop.
The correct answer should have a meaning which fits the context.

Pages 10-11 — Prefixes and Suffixes

1 a) The baby polar bear is so **adorable**.
   b) I was trying to be **helpful** when I washed the dishes.
   c) The ball hit Kayley and knocked her **unconscious**.
   d) Lyla's feeling of **happiness** increased when she found her shoes.
The prefix and suffixes which have been added all fit the context of the sentences.

Pages 12-13 — Silent Letters and Double Letters

1 a) I **maintained** a comfortable position for the whole journey.
   b) You need to wear more **clothes** in winter to keep warm.
   c) My **interesting** entry will win the competition tomorrow.
Make sure that double letters have been used correctly.

2 a) Everyone agreed that the charity event had been **successful**.
   b) While we're in London, we want to visit Nelson's **Column**.
   c) Sasha is the most **intelligent** girl in the class.
   d) I arrived just as the show was **beginning**.
These are the correct spellings of each word.

Pages 14-15 — Other Awkward Spellings

1 a) My car is running out of **diesel**.
   b) Zaneb went to the museum to see the **ancient** remains.
Use the rule " 'i' before 'e' except after 'c', but only when it rhymes with bee" to help you to work out the correct spellings.

2 a) The missing letter in 'desperate' is 'e'.
   b) The missing letter in 'factory' is 'o'.
   c) The missing letter in 'responsible' is 'i'.
   d) The missing letters in 'literature' are 'e' and 'a'.
These are the vowels needed to correctly spell each word.

126

Pages 16-21 — Practice Questions

1 flashes
'flash' becomes 'flashes' — often words ending
in 'sh' add 'es' to make the plural.

2 cheeses
'cheese' becomes 'cheeses' — this is a regular plural.

3 zeros
'zero' becomes 'zeros' — this is a regular plural.

4 sketches
'sketch' becomes 'sketches' — often words
ending in 'ch' add 'es' to make the plural.

5 logos
'logo' becomes 'logos' — this is a regular plural.

6 ourselves
'ourselves' is the correct spelling — often words ending
in 'f' lose the final 'f' and add 'ves' to make the plural.

7 series
'series' is the correct spelling — this is an irregular plural.

8 cavemen
'cavemen' is the correct spelling — this is an irregular plural.
The plural of 'man' is 'men'.

9 cherries
'cherries' is the correct spelling — when the letter
before the 'y' is a consonant, the 'y' is removed
and 'ies' is added to make the plural.

10 offspring
'offspring' is the correct spelling — this is an irregular plural.

11 queue
'queue' makes sense here — it means 'a line of people
waiting', whereas 'cue' means 'a signal to begin'.

12 barred
'barred' makes sense here — it is an adjective that means
'secured with bars', whereas 'bard' is an old term for a poet.

13 fazed
'fazed' makes sense here — it means 'concerned',
whereas 'phased' means 'done in stages'.

14 taut
'taut' makes sense here — it means 'tight', whereas 'taught'
means 'gave instruction about how to do something'.

15 draught
'draught' makes sense here — it means 'a cold breeze',
whereas 'draft' means 'the first version of a piece of writing'.

16 oar
'oar' makes sense here — it is a type of paddle, whereas 'or'
is a word used to introduce an alternative, and 'ore' refers to
natural material from which metal or minerals can be taken.

17 seize
'seize' makes sense here — it means 'take forcibly',
whereas 'seas' means 'bodies of salt water',
and 'sees' means 'observes through sight'.

18 preys
'preys' makes sense here — 'preys upon' means
'hunts', whereas 'prays' means 'addresses or says a
prayer', and 'praise' means 'to express approval'.

19 rapped
'rapped' makes sense here — it means 'tapped quickly and
repeatedly', whereas 'wrapped' means 'covered with paper or
other material' and 'rapt' means 'fascinated by something'.

20 peeked
'peeked' makes sense here — it means 'looked at
something quickly or secretively', whereas 'piqued'
means 'stimulated interest in something' and 'peaked'
means 'reached the highest point'.

21 mis — The word is 'misplaced'.

22 pre — The word is 'prescribe'.

23 dis — The word is 'disorder'.

24 un — The word is 'unrecognisable'.

25 re — The word is 'readjust'.

26 supervision
The suffix added is 'ion', but you also need
to remove the 'e' from 'supervise'.

27 movement
The suffix added is 'ment'.

28 reliable
The suffix added is 'able', but you also need to change the 'y'
in 'rely' to an 'i' — this is common for words ending in 'y'.

29 tranquillity
The suffix added is 'ity', but you also need
to add another 'l' to 'tranquil'.

30 ownership
The suffix added is 'ship'.

31 doubt
'dout' should be 'doubt' — it has a silent 'b'.

32 acquire
'aquire' should be 'acquire' — it has a silent 'c'.

33 breathe
'breath' should be 'breathe' — it has a silent 'e'.

34 writhed
'rithed' should be 'writhed' — it has a silent 'w'.

35 glistened
'glisened' should be 'glistened' — it has a silent 't'.

36 forbidden
'forbidden' is the correct spelling — it has a double 'd'.

37 assumed
'assumed' is the correct spelling — the root word is 'assume'.

38 excessive
'excessive' is the correct spelling — the root word is 'excess'.

39 befuddled
'befuddled' is the correct spelling — the root word is 'befuddle'.

40 summoned
'summoned' is the correct spelling
— the root word is 'summon'.

41 ie
The word is 'retrieve'. The vowel sound rhymes with
'bee', and it is not after 'c', so 'i' comes before 'e'.

42 ei
The word is 'feigned'. The vowel sound does not rhyme with 'bee', so 'e' comes before 'i'.

43 ie
The word is 'mischievous'. The vowel sound rhymes with 'bee' and it's not after 'c', so 'i' comes before 'e'.

44 ei
The word is 'leisurely'. The vowel sound does not rhyme with 'bee', so 'e' comes before 'i'.

45 ie
The word is 'conscience'. The vowel sound comes after 'c', but it does not rhyme with bee, so 'i' comes before 'e'.

46 description
'description' is the correct spelling
— the root word is 'describe'.

47 preference
'preference' is the correct spelling — the suffix added is 'ence'.

48 handsome
'handsome' is the correct spelling — it has a silent 'd'.

49 harmony
'harmony' is the correct spelling — the 'o' is unstressed.

50 memorable
'memorable' is the correct spelling — the suffix added is 'able', but you also need to remove the 'y' from 'memory'.

51 broach
'broach' makes sense here — it means 'bring up a topic to discuss', whereas a 'brooch' is a piece of jewellery fastened to clothing with a pin.

52 scarves
'scarves' is the correct spelling — this is an irregular plural.

53 formerly
'formerly' makes sense here — it means 'previously', whereas 'formally' means 'done in an official way'.

54 frightening
'frightening' is the correct spelling — the 'e' is unstressed.

55 observant
'observant' is the correct spelling — the root word is 'observe'.

56 accessories
'accesories' should be 'accessories' — it has a double 's'.

57 aggression
'agression' should be 'aggression' — it has a double 'g'.

58 gnarled
'narled' should be 'gnarled' — it has a silent 'g'.

59 ascent
'asent' should be 'ascent' — it has a silent 'c'.

60 subtle
'sutle' should be 'subtle' — it has a silent 'b'.

Section Two — Word Meanings

Pages 22-23 — Preparing for Word Meaning Questions

1 a) 'sang' is a verb
   b) 'honesty' is a noun (an abstract noun)
   c) 'nosy' is an adjective
   d) 'tighten' is a verb
   e) 'cryptic' is an adjective
   f) 'play' can either be a verb or a noun
   g) 'vacantly' is an adverb
   h) 'talent' is a noun (an abstract noun)

2 a) 'truth' is an abstract noun that means 'the reality of a matter'.
   b) 'cantankerous' is an adjective that means 'grumpy' or 'disagreeable'.
   c) 'wrathfully' is an adverb that means 'angrily'.
   d) 'bemusement' is a noun that means 'confusion'.
Verbs are doing words, nouns are things, adjectives describe nouns and adverbs describe verbs.

Pages 24-25 — Multiple Meanings

1 a) **talk**
'talk' can mean 'a presentation' or 'to converse'.
   b) **run**
'run' can mean 'to be in charge' or 'to move quickly'.
   c) **book**
'book' can mean 'to arrange something' or 'something you read'.

Pages 26-29 — Closest Meaning

1 a) **petrified**
Both of these mean 'very scared'.
   b) **track**
Both of these mean 'a path' or 'to follow something'
   c) **beamed**
Both of these mean 'grinned'.

2 a) **lamp**
   b) **tale**
   c) **leap**
Look at the letters you're given and think about whether the missing letters are more likely to be vowels or consonants. In the example of 'lamp', you know 'l' is rarely followed by a consonant at the start of a word, so the second letter must be a vowel.

Pages 30-33 — Opposite Meaning

1 a) **absent**
'present' means 'here', whereas 'absent' means 'away'

   b) **defend**
'accuse' means 'to blame someone', whereas
'defend' means 'to argue someone's case'.

2 a) l**ate**

   b) r**igh**t

   c) **soft**
The letters in bold are the missing letters.

Pages 34-35 — Odd One Out

1 **peaceful**
The other three all mean 'boring'.

2 **novel**
The other three are non-fiction texts.

3 **dormant**
The other three all mean 'feeling tired'.

4 **morose**
The other three all mean 'happy'.

Pages 36-37 — Reorder Words to Make a Sentence

*Your child might have made a different sentence
using the words given. This is fine, as long
as the correct word has been chosen.*

1 **are**
The words can be rearranged into the sentence
'Jo is the happiest girl I know'.

2 **rock**
The words can be rearranged into the sentence
'The walrus dived into the sea and caught a fish'.

3 **field**
The words can be rearranged into the sentence
'Take the footpath if you want to get there quickly'.

Pages 38-43 — Practice Questions

1 **school**
'school' can mean 'a place where students
are educated' or 'to teach'.

2 **confront**
'confront' can mean 'to question the validity of something'
or 'to deal with something'.

3 **whisper**
'whisper' can mean 'a hint of something' or 'to speak quietly'.

4 **light**
'light' can mean 'very bright' or 'to set something on fire'.

5 **bother**
'bother' can mean 'a trouble or difficulty' or 'to irritate'.

6 **clouded**
'clouded' can mean 'made less clear' or 'dark and gloomy'.

7 **missing**
'missing' can mean 'not having something that
you need or want' or 'unable to be found'.

8 **offer**
'offer' can mean 'to supply' or 'to present to someone'.

9 **pen**
'pen' can mean 'a place where animals are kept' or
'to write something'.

10 **wonder**
'wonder' can mean 'an amazing thing' or
'a feeling or state of amazement'.

11 **merit**
'merit' can mean 'to be worthy of something' or
'a praiseworthy quality'.

12 **station**
'station' can mean 'a place where a train or bus stops' or
'to place at a specific location'.

13 **clutch**
Both words mean 'to grip tightly'.

14 **continuous**
Both words mean 'without end'.

15 **oppose**
Both words mean 'to argue against'.

16 **technique**
Both words mean 'a way of doing something'.

17 **range**
Both words mean 'the area covered by something'.

18 **detain**
Both words mean 'to hold someone or something back'.

19 **stoop**
Both words mean 'to duck down'.

20 **exhaustive**
Both words mean 'thorough'.

21 **granule**
Both words mean 'a small piece of something'.

22 **bold**
Both words mean 'overfamiliar in social situations'.

23 **retract**
Both words mean 'to take something back'.

24 **loiter**
Both words mean 'to wait around aimlessly'.

25 **assess**
Both words mean 'to evaluate'.

26 **outlook**
Both words mean 'point of view'.

27 **endure**
Both words mean 'to put up with'.

28 **puncture**
Both words mean 'to pierce'.

29 **turmoil**
Both words mean 'a state of agitation'.

30 **conceal**
'expose' means 'to reveal', whereas
'conceal' means 'to cover up'.

31 **recede**
'approach' means 'to go towards', whereas
'recede' means 'to move away from'.

32 **harmony**
'conflict' means 'disagreement', whereas
'harmony' means 'agreement'.

Answers

33 routine
'unusual' means 'not ordinary', whereas
'routine' means 'ordinary'.

34 ashen
'flushed' means 'having red and hot skin', whereas
'ashen' means 'having very pale skin'.

35 devastated
'overjoyed' means 'extremely happy', whereas
'devastated' means 'extremely sad'.

36 adversary
'ally' means 'someone who cooperates with
someone else', whereas 'adversary' means
'someone who works against someone else'.

37 imperative
'inessential' means 'not crucial', whereas
'imperative' means 'crucial'.

38 prevalent
'uncommon' means 'not common', whereas
'prevalent' means 'widespread'.

39 overdue
'premature' means 'early', whereas 'overdue' means 'late.'

40 dispirit
'encourage' means 'to give support or confidence to someone',
whereas 'dispirit' means 'to cause someone to lose confidence'.

41 obsolete
'current' means 'something that exists or is used now',
whereas 'obsolete' means 'something that is no longer used'.

42 implant
'extract' means 'take out', whereas 'implant' means 'put in'.

43 unstable
'secure' means 'stable', whereas 'unstable' means 'not stable'.

44 advantage
'liability' means 'something that causes a disadvantage ',
whereas 'advantage' means 'something that is beneficial'.

45 tuneless
'melodious' means 'pleasant sounding', whereas
'tuneless' means 'not pleasant sounding'.

46 grateful
'unappreciative' means 'not grateful', whereas
'grateful' means 'showing or feeling appreciation'.

47 subordinate
The other three are positions of leadership.

48 hurdle
The other three refer to a sudden increase.

49 complain
The other three mean 'to express grief'.

50 therapy
The other three are words associated with illness.

51 speciality
The other three mean 'self-control'.

52 morsel
The other three mean 'a large piece of something'.

53 defeat
The other three mean 'to cause disgust or revulsion'.

54 barren
The other three are used to describe something
that is useless or ineffective.

55 hushed
The other three mean 'not spoken'.

56 chafe
The other three mean 'to make a cut or opening in something'.

57 professional
The other three mean 'skill'.

58 timidity
The other three mean 'worry'.

59 moon
The words can be rearranged into the sentence
'The astronaut floats happily inside her spaceship.'

60 trainer
The words can be rearranged into the sentence
'The determined athletes run miles every day.'

61 ribbon
The words can be rearranged into the sentence
'She gave me a beautiful bouquet of flowers.'

62 be
The words can be rearranged into the sentence
'I am going to travel the world one day.'

63 part
The words can be rearranged into the sentence
'My step-sister is a soldier in the army.'

64 learned
The words can be rearranged into the sentence
'Mateo can speak Spanish and English fluently.'

65 repair
The words can be rearranged into the sentence
'Our rusty car broke down on the motorway.'

66 are
The words can be rearranged into the sentence
'I went skydiving when we were holidaying in Thailand.'

67 inside
The words can be rearranged into the sentence
'The curious rat scampered along the empty street.'

68 will
The words can be rearranged into the sentence
'Penny has almost finished writing her second novel.'

69 icing
The words can be rearranged into the sentence
'He is planning to bake a chocolate cake tonight.'

70 falls
The words can be rearranged into the sentence
'Joe exclaimed when he tripped over the protruding rock.'

Section Three — Completing Passages

Pages 44-45 — Preparing for Cloze Questions

1 a) It was getting **dark**, so I turned on the light.

b) Stella fell off the camel and **landed** on her feet.

c) Playing basketball **improves** your coordination.

The words in bold are the correct answers.

2 a) Chen and Beth ran away from the **ug**ly monster.

b) I go swimming with my **frie**nds every Monday night.

c) My dog won't stop scratching — I think he has **flea**s.

The letters in bold are the missing letters.

Pages 46-47 — Using Rules of English — Verbs

1 a) Sadie has **eaten** all of my popcorn.

b) I have **been** to South Africa on holiday.

c) Barry's knee is **hurting** after he fell over.

d) You should **go** home or you'll be late.

e) What time do you think you will **arrive**?

f) The dolphin is about to **leap** out of the water.

The words in bold are the correct answers. Read the sentence out loud to help you find the right answer.

Pages 48-49 — Using Rules of English — Conjunctions

1 The Amazon Rainforest covers 40% of South America, <u>although</u> it has decreased in size. Humans have cut down the trees <u>because</u> they need wood for construction <u>and</u> space for farms. Conservation efforts are under way to protect the rainforest <u>and</u> stop people from illegally cutting down the trees.

The words that are underlined are the conjunctions.

2 a) I often eat cereal for breakfast **but** I sometimes eat toast.

b) I'd like to go out to the Italian restaurant tonight, **although** Chinese is my favourite.

The words in bold are the correct answers.
Look at the context to find the right conjunction.

Pages 50-53 — Answering Cloze Questions

1 At **up** to thirty metres long, blue whales are **approximately** three times the **length** of a double-decker bus. These **colossal** marine mammals eat four to eight tonnes of krill, tiny sea creatures, **every** day. Blue whales have a fringe of fine plates **attached** to their upper jaw. To feed, they **take** in a huge mouthful of water and force it out **through** the fringe. The krill are too **big** to pass between the plates, **so** they stay in the whale's mouth.

The words in bold are the correct answers.

2 With a groan, the sol**d**ier came to. His head felt as th**ough** someone had been using it as a football. With a grunt of p**ain**, he scrambled to his feet and wait**ed** for the sky to stop its alarming spinning. He bent slowly and picked up his rifle, then stumbled **on**ward. His in**j**ured ankle made it difficult to walk quickly, but he knew he had to reach the trench before the next round of shelling st**a**rted. Just a few more paces and he would reach safety and s**h**elter.

The letters in bold are the missing letters.

Pages 54-61 — Practice Questions

1 **has**
The sentence should be 'The storm **has** blown down the fence.'

2 **of**
The sentence should be 'We had a good time in spite **of** the terrible music.'

3 **treading**
The sentence should be 'Fiona was **treading** water for a long time.'

4 **so**
The sentence should be 'The hamster hoarded the food **so** he could eat it later.'

5 **wrote**
The sentence should be 'The author who **wrote** this book is a genius.'

6 **Although**
The sentence should be '**Although** it was hot, I took my coat.'

7 **choose**
The sentence should be 'He was asked to **choose** his favourite flavour.'

8 **whenever**
The sentence should be 'Mel made carrot cake **whenever** Afiya came to visit.'

9 **woke**
The sentence should be 'Timo accidentally **woke** up his baby sister.'

10 **or**
The sentence should be 'We could either record the song again **or** leave it as it is.'

11 **flown**
The sentence should be 'The pilot has **flown** on hundreds of planes.'

12 **Besides**
The sentence should be '**Besides** going swimming, Camila likes riding her bike.'

13 **discipline**
'the **discipline** is actually thousands of years old'

14 **originating**
'**originating** in ancient India'

15 **refers**
'the term 'yoga' **refers** to a set of spiritual and physical practices'

16 **form**
'a **form** of exercise'

17 **develop**
'to **develop** flexibility and strength'

18 **infiltrated**
'a sense of unease **infiltrated** the camp'

19 **scout**
'Ethan had left to **scout** around the jungle'

20 **emanating**
'An ominous rustling **emanating** from the undergrowth'

21 **caught**
'**caught** the explorers unawares'

Answers

22 apprehensively
'they clung **apprehensively** to one another'

23 symbol
'a **symbol** of Australia'

24 primarily
'move around **primarily** by hopping'

25 admired
'While kangaroos are **admired** by tourists'

26 pest
'often regarded as a **pest**'

27 booming
'their **booming** population'

28 heralded
'is often **heralded** as the world's southernmost city'

29 accordingly
'**accordingly**, one train to Ushuaia has been named 'The End of the World Train''

30 undeserving
'Ushuaia is **undeserving** of this accolade'

31 classed
'which is **classed** as a city in Chile'

32 marginally
'**marginally** further south'

33 acute
'an **acute** feeling of claustrophobia'

34 favouring
'**favouring** the slower-paced life'

35 sweeping
'**sweeping** landscapes'

36 strode
'as she **strode** on'

37 gaining
'she felt herself **gaining** in confidence'

38 notorious
'it is **notorious** for causing bad breath'

39 insufficient
'there is **insufficient** evidence'

40 superstition
'According to **superstition**'

41 ward
'this food can **ward** off vampires'

42 popularised
'an idea which was **popularised** by a famous novel'

43 glazed
'Thandiwe's eyes **glazed** over'

44 Truthfully
'**Truthfully**, she was envious'

45 impeded
'Her attempt to get a ticket had been **impeded**'

46 fabricating
'Just as Thandiwe was **fabricating** an excuse'

47 rummaged
'Tim **rummaged** around in his bag'

48 Budding
'**Budding** mountaineers might be surprised to learn'

49 acknowledged
'are **acknowledged** to be'

50 treacherous
'more **treacherous**'

51 descending
'successfully **descending** K2 on skis'

52 astonishment
'much to the **astonishment** of his peers'

53 expanses
'Salt flats are vast **expanses** of salt and minerals'

54 breathtaking
'Perhaps the most **breathtaking** example is Salar de Uyuni'

55 reflects
'the ground behaves like a mirror and **reflects** its surroundings'

56 venture
'Many people **venture** out to experience the wonder'

57 underneath
'seeing clouds **underneath** their feet'

58 eternity
'After what felt like an **eternity**'

59 immersed
'As soon as she was **immersed** in the water'

60 vibrant
'a **vibrant** world of multicoloured coral'

61 shimmered
'whose scales **shimmered** in the sunlight'

62 marvel
'she had all summer to **marvel** at it'

63 expeditions
'an explorer who led **expeditions**'

64 Together
'**Together** with his team'

65 challenge
'the **challenge** of becoming the first man to reach the South Pole'

66 contend
'Scott had to **contend** with fierce weather'

67 striving
'**striving** to get there first'

68 lowered
'Milo **lowered** himself into his seat'

69 increased
'the plane's speed rapidly **increased**'

70 curiosity
'his **curiosity** got the better of him'

71 shrinking
'**shrinking** to the size of ants'

72 entire
'he could see the **entire** world'

73 regard
'are held in a high **regard**'

74 admiration
'just as worthy of **admiration**'

75 identical
'almost **identical** to the face of a primate'

76 exploding
'resemble an **exploding** firework'

77 thrive
'can even **thrive** in environments destroyed by fire'

78 averse
'had always been **averse** to confrontation'

79 argument
'She rarely had an **argument**'

80 devised
'she had **devised**'

81 foolproof
'a **foolproof** plan'

82 anticipating
'her brother definitely wouldn't be **anticipating** it'

83 luxuries
'one of life's **luxuries**'

84 origin
'Although the **origin** of ice cream is unknown'

85 historians
'**historians** have found evidence'

86 gathering
'it was made by **gathering** various fruits'

87 combining
'made by **combining** buffalo milk with other ingredients'

88 whirring
'The sound of the rocket's engine **whirring**'

89 abyss
'the dark **abyss**'

90 resumed
'she **resumed** plotting her route'

91 intercepted
'It had **intercepted** an enemy transmission'

92 pursuers
'her **pursuers** had picked up her trail'

93 lurking
'**lurking** in the depths of the ocean'

94 attempted
'Scientists have **attempted** to study these creatures for years'

95 limited
'a **limited** amount of data'

96 consider
'when you **consider** that'

97 advanced
'highly **advanced** underwater technology'

Section Four — Comprehension

Pages 62-63 — Reading the Text

1 a) Eric Debuski's stage name is Lavahead.

   b) Joaquin works in a shop — in the passage it says that "he scanned through Eric's basket", which means that he was working on a till.

   c) Joaquin stutters and Eric tells him to shut his mouth, probably because he is gaping. This shows he is feeling nervous. The text also says "it was astounding", which shows how thrilled Joaquin was.

Try to mention all of the relevant information when you're writing an answer to a comprehension question.

Pages 66-67 — Finding Hidden Facts

1 **Marta**
Marta sees a pedestrian, a cat, a tractor and a cyclist.

2 **Four**
Glen is the only child who does not see a motorised vehicle. Kim and Luca see a car, Marta sees a tractor and Ali sees both.

Pages 68-70 — Understanding the Language in the Text

1 **B**
The phrase "the sky caught fire" describes the colour of the sky. You can tell that it is sunset because the passage says 'the burning orb [the Sun] plunged into the ocean'.

Pages 71-73 — Multiple Statement Questions — Logic

1 **D**
Nathan beat Li, and Li beat Zach. Zach didn't come last, and he can't have come fourth because Mike came fourth. This means that Zach must have come third and Li must have come second.

Pages 74-75 — Word Meanings

1 **A**
'Fervently' means 'with great passion or emotion'.

2 **D**
'Circumspect' means 'aware of possible consequences', which is closest in meaning to 'cautious'.

Pages 76-77 — Reasoning Questions

1 **B**
The writer asks "Where were they?" and says that Isla "scanned the horizon feverishly". This shows how anxious Isla was, which makes the reader feel worried too.

Pages 80-87 — Practice Questions

1 Jorge
Jorge has four toppings: tomato, onions, cheese and bacon.

2 Uri
Uri has only been to Manchester.

3 Sona
Sona does four hobbies: swimming, hockey, boxing and cycling.

4 Bianca
Bianca likes four genres: comedy, horror, romance and action.

5 Shirley
Shirley is only using two colours: white and blue.

6 Ella
Ella helps out in four rooms: the kitchen, lounge, dining room and garage.

7 Anders
Anders brought five types of food: crisps, sandwiches, sausage rolls, cookies and brownies.

8 Victor
Victor only bought two types of fruit: apples and peaches.

9 A
Luca collected the second highest number of shells, and Jasper collected more shells than Luca. This means that Jasper must have collected the most shells.

10 D
Li has two pets. Petra has twice as many pets as Li, which means she has four. Maria has one fewer pet than Petra, so she has three. Craig and Naomi both have the same number of pets as Maria, which means they have three. This means Naomi has more pets than Li.

11 B
Ellie comes third. Anza doesn't come fourth but beats Orla, which means Anza must come first or second. John beats Anza, which means he must come first and Anza must come second. This means Orla must come fourth or fifth, so she can't have beaten Ellie.

12 D
Luke got on the bus at 5.45. Anthony got on twenty minutes after Luke, which means he got on at 6.05. Jessie got on ten minutes after Anthony, which means she got on at 6.15. Luke got on the bus half an hour before Summer, which means Summer got on at 6.15 too. This means Jessie and Summer got on at the same time.

13 B
There are six apples. Between them, Bella, Ray and Gemma eat five apples. This means Denny can't have eaten two apples and a pear, because there is only one apple left.

14 C
Rachel scored 75 marks, which was five marks more than Ash. This means Ash scored 70. Ash scored fifteen marks fewer than Thandi, so Thandi must have scored 85.

15 A
"proceed from" means 'come from'.

16 C
"wrathfully" means 'furiously'.

17 B
"dismay" can mean 'alarm'.

18 C
If something is 'winging it's way', it is travelling very quickly. Therefore, the phrase "fear winged his steps" suggests that Jonas is running quickly because he is afraid of being caught.

19 D
Line 1 states that Aurelia was twelve years old when her mum discovered the tomb, and in line 5, Aurelia says the discovery happened "four years ago to the day". Therefore, Aurelia must now be sixteen years old.

20 A
In lines 10-11, just after Aurelia's mum pulls her back, sand starts to "flow into a hole in the ground". This suggests Aurelia's mum was pulling her away from the hole so that she wouldn't be swept in.

21 C
The phrase "twiddling my thumbs" is used to show that someone has nothing to do or is waiting for something to happen. This suggests that Aurelia is bored because she has nothing to do while her mum takes equipment into the tomb.

22 B
It was "Not long after midday" (line 8) when Aurelia's mum found the tunnel, and it took Aurelia's mum's team the "next three hours" (line 14) to get the equipment into the tomb. Therefore, it must have been after two o'clock in the afternoon when Aurelia entered the tunnel.

23 B
"sporadically" means 'intermittently'.

24 C
When people are afraid, they might shiver or shake gently. Aurelia steps "tentatively" into the tunnel, which means that she goes inside cautiously. She also moves "closer" (line 19) to her mum and her eyes are described as "darting around" (line 20), as she enters the tunnel. This suggests that she shivers because she is feeling uneasy.

25 B
"sentries" is another word for 'guards', so this suggests that the statues look like they are guarding the stone box that they are standing over.

26 D
The statues in the tomb are described as "three times" (line 26) Aurelia's height, which means the ceiling must be at least three times taller than she is.

27 D
If someone feels as though they have 'stepped back in time', it means they feel like they have gone into the past. Therefore, Aurelia's comment suggests that the tomb appears untouched and is much the same as it was in Ancient Egyptian times.

28 C
To be 'in awe' of something means to be amazed or astonished by it. Aurelia's "mouth fell open" (line 28) when her mum told her the age of the tomb, which suggests that Aurelia is amazed.

Mixed Practice Tests

Pages 88-90 — Mixed Practice Test 1

1   D
In line 4, the kite expresses "self-admiration".
This suggests it is feeling confident.

2   C
To be in awe of something means to be impressed
by it. The kite says the crowds "Admire my flight
above the steeple" (line 6), which suggests that the
kite thinks they are impressed by its flight.

3   A
In lines 9-10, the kite states that if it was "free" it would
"take a flight" above the clouds. Line 12 states that the kite's
string "confines" it "near the ground", which means that
the string is stopping the kite from going higher. In line 14,
the kite hopes to "fly without a string". This suggests that
the kite wants to be free of its string so it can fly freely.

4   D
To 'brave' something means to risk it. Therefore, the
kite is suggesting that it would be willing to face a
dangerous bird of prey if it meant it could be free.

5   C
Line 20 states that the kite "fluttered downwards".
If something 'flutters down' this suggest that
it falls in an irregular, unsteady way.

6   D
Line 6 refers to a "steeple", which is another name
for a church tower. Line 13 refers to an eagle,
which is a type of bird. Line 22 describes the kite
landing "in the tide". Tides are the movements of the
sea. There is no mention of a jail in the poem.

7   B
"elevation" can mean 'altitude'.

8   C
"in vain" can mean 'without success'.

9   momentary
'perpetual' means 'occurring continuously', whereas
'momentary' means 'occurring very briefly'.

10 comply
'disobey' means 'to go against orders',
whereas 'comply' means 'to obey'.

11 uninterested
'inquisitive' means 'curious', whereas
'uninterested' means 'not curious'.

12 apathetic
'passionate' means 'enthusiastic about something',
whereas 'apathetic' means 'showing no interest'.

13 stationary
'mobile' means 'moving', whereas 'stationary' means 'still'.

14 cooperative
'quarrelsome' means 'prone to arguing', whereas 'cooperative'
means 'willing or able to work with others'.

15 outlandish
Both words mean 'strange'.

16 mystifying
Both words mean 'difficult to understand'.

17 opportune
Both words mean 'advantageous'.

18 perturb
Both words mean 'to cause upset or worry'.

19 immune
Both words mean 'protected from
being affected by something'.

20 divulge
Both words mean 'to reveal'.

21 strident
Both words can mean 'unpleasant and grating'.

Pages 91-93 — Mixed Practice Test 2

1   preference
The other three refer to something
that is done on a regular basis.

2   dictionary
The other three are types of fictional writing.

3   searing
The other three mean 'giving off light'.

4   nourished
The other three mean 'ate quickly'.

5   arrow
The other three are projectiles that are
usually thrown using your hand.

6   repugnant
'attractive' means 'appealing', whereas
'repugnant' means 'very unappealing'.

7   delay
'expedite' means 'to speed something up', whereas
'delay' means 'to slow something down'.

8   gullible
'sceptical' means 'difficult to convince', whereas
'gullible' means 'easily convinced'.

9   authentic
'counterfeit' means 'fake', whereas
'authentic' means 'genuine'.

10 admonish
'praise' means 'to express approval', whereas 'admonish'
means 'to express disapproval of someone's actions'.

11 rain
The words can be rearranged into the sentence
'The mud squelched loudly under my shoes'.

12 until
The words can be rearranged into the sentence
'Three cheetahs sprinted determinedly across the savannah'.

13 after
The words can be rearranged into the sentence
'The storm seemed to be abating slowly'.

14 which
The words can be rearranged into the sentence
'Anna refused to relinquish her favourite book'.

15 spreading
'**spreading** to the rest of her body'

16 loomed
'Dark trees **loomed** all around her'

17 burden
'drooping under the **burden** of the snow'

18 fading
'The light was **fading** quickly'

19 undeniably
'but she was **undeniably** lost'

20 normal
'she had taken her **normal** route'

21 Unfortunately
'**Unfortunately**, a blizzard had begun soon afterwards'

22 obscured
'the snow had **obscured** the trail'

23 danger
'to get herself out of **danger**'

24 contrasting
'the stillness of the forest **contrasting** with the harsh sound'

25 attention
'A noise had attracted her **attention**'

26 identify
'she could **identify** it easily'

27 exertion
'her muscles burning from the **exertion**'

28 into
'the forest opened up **into** a clearing'

Pages 94-96 — Mixed Practice Test 3

1 C
If something travels 'at the speed of sound', it travels at the same speed that sound moves through the air. The ISS travels "more than twenty times" as fast as sound, which means that it travels incredibly quickly.

2 D
Lines 4-5 state that the ISS orbits the Earth "every ninety minutes", and astronauts see the sun rise "sixteen times a day". Therefore, the ISS only circles Earth sixteen times every twenty-four hours.

3 D
If someone is a "test subject" this means they are having experiments performed on them. Lines 10-11 state that, while the astronauts are in space, scientists back on Earth are "monitor how life in space affects their health". 'monitor' means 'observe'.

4 C
Lines 15-16 state that there is "no air and very little gravity" in space, so experiments carried out in space have "very different outcomes" than they would on Earth. This suggests that astronauts set up experiments outside to learn more about the effects of these different conditions.

5 B
Lines 21-22 state that the suits "provide the astronaut with oxygen to breathe". Lines 23-24 state that the astronauts can use the thruster in their spacesuit to "propel themselves back to the station" if their tether fails, showing that spacesuits can help astronauts return to the station in an emergency. Line 19 states that the suits protect astronauts from "huge fluctuations in temperature". There is no mention of spacesuits being used to travel between the ISS and spaceships.

6 A
Line 19 states that the spacesuits protect the astronauts from "huge fluctuations in temperature" in space. Lines 19-20 state that temperatures can reach 120 °C in direct sunlight, and lines 20-21 state that temperatures in the shade can be −150 °C. This shows that the spacesuits can withstand both very hot and very cold temperatures.

7 C
"ground-breaking" means 'cutting-edge'.

8 A
"sophisticated" means 'advanced'.

9 sullied
'pristine' means 'unspoilt', whereas 'sullied' means 'dirtied'.

10 abhor
'adore' means 'to love', whereas 'abhor' means 'to hate'.

11 shunned
'welcomed' can mean 'accepted gladly', whereas 'shunned' means 'rejected'.

12 operational
'broken' means 'not working' whereas 'operational' means 'working as intended'.

13 disadvantageous
'favourable' means 'advantageous', whereas 'disadvantageous' means 'unfavourable'.

14 introverted
'outgoing' means 'confident', whereas 'introverted' can mean 'reserved'.

15 dispensable
'required' means 'needed', whereas 'dispensable' means 'not needed'.

16 rotten
'rotten' can mean 'dishonest and immoral' or 'mouldy and decayed'.

17 crush
'crush' can mean 'to compress' or 'a large group of people tightly packed together'.

18 serious
'serious' can mean 'earnest' or 'of great importance'.

19 contrary
'contrary' can mean 'prone to disagreeing with people' or 'in opposition to something else'.

20 remedy
'remedy' can mean 'a treatment for an illness' or 'to put something right'.

21 build
'build' can mean 'to construct something' or 'the shape of someone's body'.

1 D

In lines 3-4, Jamie wonders why he should "have to vie for his parents' attention". To 'vie for' something means to 'compete for' it, so this suggests that Jamie is worried that he will have to compete with his sister for his parents' time and attention.

2 D

Lines 14-15 state that Jamie's grandma has noticed "Jamie's mood", suggesting that she has realised he is not feeling happy about his sister's birth. Immediately after this, she suggests that they buy the flowers. This suggests that she wants Jamie to join in with the celebration by giving him a chance to pick the flowers.

3 B

When Jamie sees his sister, he exclaims "She's got the same colour eyes as me!" (line 22), which suggests he's interested in the similarities between them. In line 24, Jamie sits down "Immediately" when his mum asks if he'd like to hold his sister, showing how eager he is to see her more closely.

4 C

"imminent" can mean 'approaching'.

5 commandeer

Both words mean 'to take control of'.

6 worship

Both words mean 'to show strong admiration for something or someone'.

7 optimal

Both words mean 'perfect'.

8 infringe

Both words mean 'to cross a boundary without permission'.

9 righteous

Both words mean 'virtuous'.

10 natural

Both words can mean 'related to living things'.

11 scan

Both words mean 'to read something quickly'.

12 introduced

'settlers from Ireland **introduced** their language'

13 evolved

'Gaelic **evolved** over centuries'

14 widespread

'became **widespread** throughout the country'

15 steeply

'began to decline **steeply**'

16 authorities

'the **authorities** suppressed the use of Scottish Gaelic'

17 punished

'children could even be **punished** for using the language at school'

18 recent

'In **recent** years'

19 revive

'the Scottish government has attempted to **revive** the language'

20 visible

'Scottish Gaelic has been made more **visible**'

21 offer

'A number of schools now **offer** teaching'

22 appreciation

'an **appreciation** of both languages'

23 broadcast

'some television channels and radio stations **broadcast** in Scottish Gaelic'

24 objective

'The government's **objective** is'

25 speakers

'to increase the number of Scottish Gaelic **speakers**'

Test-Style Papers

1 C

'intimidating' means 'frightening'. Line 7 states that the house is "hospitable-looking", and in line 8 there is a "cheerful glimmer" coming from the house. This suggests that the house appears warm and welcoming, so it cannot be intimidating.

2 D

In line 5, Nat is "cheered" when the man at the gate tells him that the lady of the house will help him. He also says that he "felt that it was hardly possible" that the comforts of the house could be for him (lines 10-11), and he knocks on the door with a "timid rap" (line 12), which shows he is nervous. This suggests that, while Nat is hopeful of receiving help at the house, he is also feeling uncertain about what will happen.

3 A

Line 15 states that the servant-maid "seemed used to receiving strange boys", which suggests that it is normal for a boy like Nat to arrive at Plumfield.

4 C

The servant-maid tells Nat to "Sit there and drip on the mat" (line 16), which suggests that his clothes are wet, and he needs to dry off. The servant-maid goes on to say "while I take this [the letter] in to missis" (line 16) which suggests that she wants Nat to remain seated until the "missis" is ready to see him.

5 A

If a place is "swarming", it means that it's overrun with moving people or things. Therefore, the phrase "swarming with boys" suggests that the house is full of boys.

6 D

Line 19 states that it is "twilight". This is the period of evening between daylight and darkness. In line 21, the boys are "in all stages of evening relaxation". This shows that it is evening when Nat arrives at the house.

7 A

Line 34 mentions "a girl singing a lullaby". Line 28 mentions someone "caricaturing" members of the household, which means they were drawing amusing pictures. Line 32 mentions "a brisk game of tag" on the landing. There is no mention of anyone eating.

8 C

An 'inviting prospect' is something that is interesting or attractive to someone. The hall is described as the "most inviting prospect of all", which suggests Nat is more interested in what's happening in the hall than anywhere else.

9 B

Lines 39-40 state that Tommy's head had been "rendered nearly as hard as a cannon-ball by eleven years of constant bumping". This shows that Tommy must be at least eleven years old.

10 B

When Tommy realises that Nat is new to the house, he remembers "the duties of hospitality" (line 49) and invites Nat to play with him. If someone shows 'hospitality', it means they are making a guest or stranger feel welcome.

11 D

Although Nat wants to join in, he says that he won't until he knows whether he's "going to stay or not" (line 50).

12 C

Line 3 states that Nat has "got a letter for the lady" and that "Mr Laurence" has sent Nat there. In line 47, Nat tells Tommy that his surname is "Blake". There is no mention of whether Nat will stay at Plumfield by the end of the passage.

13 C

'tantalising' means 'tempting'.

14 B

'detriment' can mean 'damage'.

15 C

'unabated relish' means 'undiminished enjoyment'.

16 B

'soberly' means 'quietly and seriously'.

17 sit

The words can be rearranged into the sentence 'We went to the park for a picnic.'

18 lack

The words can be rearranged into the sentence 'The plant could not grow without enough water.'

19 for

The words can be rearranged into the sentence 'Suzie thought hard about joining a new football team.'

20 write

The words can be rearranged into the sentence 'Remember to give your neighbour their post.'

21 run

The words can be rearranged into the sentence 'The dog began to chase a squirrel.'

22 evenings

The words can be rearranged into the sentence 'Arthur failed to lock the window last night.'

23 took

The words can be rearranged into the sentence 'The surfer got lost on her journey to the seaside.'

24 slices

The words can be rearranged into the sentence 'Try a bite of this chocolate cake.'

25 validate

Both words mean 'to show that something is true'.

26 marooned

Both words mean 'left or trapped somewhere'.

27 story

Both words can mean 'a long tale'.

28 permitted

Both words mean 'officially allowed to do something'.

29 liable

Both words mean 'likely to do something'.

30 lure

Both words mean 'to tempt'.

31 embellished

Both words mean 'decorated with extra features or details'.

32 assemblage

Both words mean 'a group of things'.

33 subordinate

Both words mean 'of a lower rank'.

34 implement

Both words mean 'to put into effect'.

35 heal

'injure' means 'to cause harm', whereas 'heal' means 'to cure'.

36 understand

'misapprehend' means 'to misunderstand', whereas 'understand' means 'to interpret correctly'.

37 virtuous

'evil' means 'immoral', whereas 'virtuous' means 'moral'.

38 quarrel

'concur' means 'to agree', whereas 'quarrel' means 'to disagree'.

39 hostile

'friendly' means 'welcoming', whereas 'hostile' means 'unfriendly'.

40 mistrust

'faith' can mean 'trust in something', whereas 'mistrust' means 'a lack of trust'.

41 unjust

'fair' means 'equal and balanced', whereas 'unjust' means 'not fair'.

42 relaxed

'strict' means 'harsh and firm', whereas 'relaxed' means 'easy-going'.

43 ordinary

'phenomenal' means 'extraordinary', whereas 'ordinary' means 'normal'.

44 honest

'deceptive' means 'misleading', whereas 'honest' means 'truthful'.

45 Famed

'**Famed** for its towering walls of red rock'

46 extends

'the canyon **extends** for 277 miles'

47 draws

'The area **draws** a huge number of tourists'

48 astonishing
'to view this **astonishing** desert landscape'

49 plummet
'when temperatures **plummet** and snow lines the cliffs'

50 extensive
'The canyon also has an **extensive** history'

51 along
'exposing distinct layers **along** the length of the canyon'

52 while
'The oldest layer of exposed rock is around two billion years old, **while** the youngest layer is'

53 only
'the youngest layer is **only** around 100 000 years old'

54 winds
'the river **winds** its way between the cliffs.'

55 partake
'Many people **partake** in river rafting experiences'

56 numerous
'walking trails provide **numerous** opportunities'

57 for
'opportunities **for** sightseeing'

58 vigilant
'hikers need to be **vigilant**'

59 pose
'there are creatures that may **pose** a threat'

60 blend
'rattlesnakes that **blend** into the surrounding rock'

Pages 112-123 — Test-Style Paper 2

1   C
Line 7 states that the tribal chief "was seen covering himself in gold dust from head to toe". Lines 7-8 state that the Spanish explorers gave the tribal chief his "legendary title" because of his "supposed penchant for gold". The phrase 'penchant for' means 'liking for', which suggests that the explorers named the chief "El Dorado" because he covered himself in gold.

2   D
If a person 'embellishes' a story, it means they have added extra details. Line 10 states that the "explorers' imaginations ran wild", and line 11 states that "El Dorado was transformed from one rich man into an entire golden city". This suggests that the explorers added details that weren't part of the original tale.

3   A
Lines 21-22 state that there is "evidence to suggest that 'The Golden One' was more than just a myth". Then, lines 22-25 refer to the account written by Juan Rodriguez Freyle, suggesting that this is the "evidence" that El Dorado wasn't just a myth. Lines 24-25 also state that Freyle's account "explained the presence of gold in Lake Guatavita".

4   D
Lines 33-34 state that the raft was discovered "some three hundred years after Freyle described the Muisca ceremony." Line 22 states that Freyle wrote about the Muisca ceremony in 1636. Therefore, the raft must have been discovered 300 years after this in the 1900s.

5   B
Line 27 states that the Muisca civilisation existed "alongside others such as the Inca and the Maya". This suggests that the Muisca, Inca and Maya were just three of several ancient American civilisations.

6   C
In line 42, the author states that "irreplaceable relics" have been lost, and that they "could have given great insight into" Muisca civilisation. This suggests that the writer is disappointed that this knowledge has been lost forever.

7   A
"fabricated" can mean 'invented'.

8   B
"commune" can mean 'converse'.

9   devour
Both words mean 'to destroy completely'.

10 falsify
Both words mean 'to make a misleading or false version of something'.

11 shared
Both words mean 'experienced by more than one person or group'.

12 demeanour
Both words mean 'someone's behaviour towards others'.

13 compliant
Both words mean 'inclined to do what is asked'.

14 authorise
Both words mean 'to allow'.

15 convoluted
Both words mean 'difficult to understand'.

16 esteemed
Both words mean 'respected'.

17 gravity
Both words can mean 'importance'.

18 recognise
Both words mean 'distinguish from something else'.

19 deny
'concede' means 'to accept the validity of something', whereas 'deny' means 'to reject the validity of something'.

20 detain
'liberate' means 'to set free', whereas 'detain' means 'to keep captive'.

21 stagnant
'active' means 'mobile', whereas 'stagnant' means 'immobile'.

22 tact
'insensitivity' means 'a lack of sensitivity', whereas 'tact' means 'sensitivity'.

23 appease
'provoke' means 'to anger', whereas 'appease' means 'to make less angry'.

24 degenerate
'improve' means 'to get better', whereas 'degenerate' means 'to get worse'.

25 imperceptible
'noticeable' means 'visible', whereas
'imperceptible' means 'invisible'.

26 beneficial
'destructive' means 'negative', whereas
'beneficial' means 'positive'.

27 understanding
'ignorance' means 'a lack of knowledge or comprehension',
whereas 'understanding' means 'comprehension'.

28 duplicity
'honesty' means 'truthfulness', whereas
'duplicity' means 'dishonesty'.

29 confer
'confer' can mean 'to have discussions' or 'to give to'.

30 means
'means' can mean 'a way of doing something' or 'means to do'.

31 deliberate
'deliberate' can mean 'to think about' or 'on purpose'.

32 distinct
'distinct' can mean 'separate' or 'well-defined'.

33 regard
'regard' can mean 'to look at' or 'esteem'.

34 progress
'progress' can mean 'to move forward' or 'forward movement'.

35 disturb
'disturb' can mean 'to upset' or 'to interfere with something'.

36 separate
'separate' can mean 'to split apart' or 'not together'.

37 harvest
The other three all mean 'to look after'.

38 bewildered
The other three all mean 'very shocked or distressed'.

39 please
The other three all mean 'to express admiration'.

40 trailer
The other three are vehicles that are powered by engines.

41 knoll
The other three describe depressions in a surface.

42 crops
The other three are types of crop.

43 fabric
The other three refer to body coverings of animals.

44 marmalade
The other three are savoury condiments.

45 saturated
The other three all mean 'contented'.

46 tide
The other three describe heavy rainfall.

47 consider
'When you **consider** getting a new pet'

48 contemplate
'Not many people would **contemplate**
the possibility of a pet rat'

49 stereotype
'due to the **stereotype** that they inhabit dark, dirty places'

50 differ
'**differ** from their sewer-dwelling cousins'

51 inquisitive
'Fancy rats are naturally **inquisitive**'

52 perform
'They can be taught to **perform** tricks'

53 obeying
'**obeying** simple commands'

54 intricate
'to solving **intricate** puzzles'

55 utilise
'fancy rats will **utilise** all the skills at their disposal'

56 energetic
'Their **energetic** nature'

57 liken
'causes some people to **liken** them to tiny dogs'

58 companions
'makes them affectionate and engaging **companions**'

59 interaction
'Human **interaction** alone isn't enough'

60 loneliness
'to prevent **loneliness**'

Index

A
adjectives 22
adverbs 22
antonyms 30-33

C
clauses 46
closest meaning 26-29
cloze 2, 44-53
comprehension 62-79
conjunctions 48, 49

D
double letters 12, 13

F
fact finding questions 64
feelings 77
fiction 62
figurative language 68-70

H
hidden facts 66, 67
homographs 8, 24
homophones 8, 9

I
'i before e' rule 14, 15
imagery 68-70
irony 69
irregular plurals 6

K
key words 63

L
literal language 68
logic 71-73

M
metaphors 69
multiple choice 1, 78
multiple meanings 24, 25
multiple-statement questions 65, 71-73

N
non-fiction 62
nouns 22

O
odd one out 34, 35
opposite meaning 30-33

P
personification 69
phrases 46
plurals 6, 7
prefixes 4, 10, 11
preparing for the 11+ 3
puns 8
purpose 76

Q
question types 2

R
reasoning questions 65, 76, 77
reordering words 36, 37

S
silent letters 12, 13
similes 68
spelling 4-15
standard answer 1, 79
suffixes 5, 10, 11
synonyms 26-29

T
tenses 46, 47

U
unstressed vowels 14

V
verbs 22, 46, 47
vocabulary 45

W
word meanings 2, 22-37, 64, 74, 75
word type 22, 23, 28, 32

VHSDE1